No Surprises
Project Management:

A Proven
Early Warning System
for Staying on
Track

[TIMM J. ESQUE]

Library of Congress Catalog Card Number: 99-066687

ACT Publishing
655 Redwood Highway, Suite 362
Mill Valley, California 94941
(415) 388-6651; (800) 995-6651; FAX (415) 388-6672
E-mail: Lila@ACTcanoe.com

Printed in the United States of America

ISBN: 1-882939-04-2, soft cover
ISBN: 1-882939-05-0, hard cover

Table of Contents

Preface

The pace of change, spurred on by technology, may be the defining characteristic of our culture as we approach the twenty-first century. The question is: Will our ever-increasing pace enable us to go farther and accomplish more, or will we just spin out of control? In organizations, the answer to this question depends primarily on learning to manage in a rocket-paced, complex environment. Successful management today means operating on the edge while maintaining enough of a sense of control to prevent sloppiness and panic. This book offers an approach to project management that has been demonstrated to accomplish this balancing act.

No Suprises Project Management is directed primarily at experienced program managers, project managers and team leaders. However, the lessons and tools should be very accessible to anyone who has participated on complex projects, and they apply to virtually any project environment. To this end, an effort has been made to include examples from project environments at varying levels of complexity.

The primary objective of this book is to provide managers in project-oriented environments with a method and tools to immediately improve performance. However, it is hoped that readers of the book will also see the potential for creating a work environment that will attract and retain the best talent available. In the 1980's, organizations that internalized the Total-Quality philosophy learned that, contrary to conventional wisdom, it is not necessary to choose between quality and productivity. Quality and productivity are complementary when managed appropriately. Thus, an intended message of this book is that there is a similar complementary relationship between productivity (which we now understand includes quality) and quality of work life. When managed appropriately, the most productive project teams are also the ones people most want to be a part of. Once again, organizations can have their cake and eat it too.

Acknowledgements

Writing this book was more an act of synthesis than creation. Although tailored to modern work environments, the methods in the book are built on the foundation of performance and management science. I will refrain from listing all the architects of performance and management science that influenced this work. However, the two that have had the most direct impact on me are the late Thomas F. Gilbert, known to some as the father of performance technology, and William R. Daniels, cofounder and senior consultant at American Consulting and Training. Allan Scherr, PhD, former IBM Fellow and now senior vice president for EMC^2, and Rick Bair, principal at JMJ Associates, greatly expanded my view of commitment and breakthrough performance. Dr. Behnam Tabrizi, associate consulting professor of Engineering Management at Stanford University, taught me to write case studies and provided enthusiasm and encouragement for my work. And, Rick Dehmel, an Intel colleague, introduced Intel and me to whole-team kickoff meetings—which he called Map Day.

The experience that convinced me of the value of commitment-based project management would not have happened without the risk taking and leadership skills of Mike LaTondre, Jerry Verseput and their respective teams in the chipset development organization at Intel Corporation. Jim Falkenstrom and Ron Smith (then general manager of the organization) were also instrumental in this success story. My good friend and Intel colleague, Ted Kastelic, was my consulting partner on these defining projects. Steve Strauss and his team helped me apply the commitment-based approach to suppliers and produced the first PAC chart. Linda Stone was another invaluable source of partnership and support.

I learned about the practical applications of performance systems on projects from many talented Intel managers and team leaders, most notably: Jeff Abramson, Steve Stevens, Harvey Jong, Guru Prasadh, Dub Dierke, Nancy Heckman, Coung Luu and Ameet Bhansali. Others who influenced the book through dialogue or feedback on the manuscript include: Bob Stensland, Kent Wickware, Mike Porter, Tracy Koon and Tom Innes from Intel; Allan Brown, Linda Rising and Sermin Boyson from AG Communications; Bill Seidman from Management Marketplace; Rick Abel from Spencer Stuart, Bryan Jobes from Boeing and Bernard Johann, PhD. Debbi LaRocque provided production support and valuable encouragement. And finally, thanks to Lila Sparks-Daniels at ACT Publishing and Graham Core and his very committed team at Professional Resources & Communications, Inc.

I dedicate this book to my mother Alice, who believed in me long before I did, and to my wife Shelly and daughter Jacquelin for being the joys of my life.

PART I

Lessons from a
Complex Environment

A Common and Vicious Cycle

The following case study is based primarily on the author's extensive work with, and observation of, the developers of a single product line at Intel Corporation. Statisticians will tell you that the only thing more reliable than a large random sample is extensive data from a single source over time (the longitudinal study). This case unfolded over a five-year period in which a complex product evolved through four generations of design.

Earlier renditions of this case have been shared with numerous product development managers and teams both within and outside of Intel. The feedback is virtually always the same—"that sounds a lot like what goes on in our organization." As you read the case, see if anything sounds familiar to you. If it does, you and your team or organization can probably benefit from the step by step methods described in the following chapters.

CASE STUDY

Good Times, Bad Times

Imagine yourself on the executive staff of a company whose products are performing well in a lucrative market sector. You are approaching an important new product launch that you are confident will ensure continued success in the market. The launch has been timed to optimize the profits of the previous generation of the product and also to ensure high demand for the new generation. Because the product is complex, this has required excellent marketing competence, and it has been difficult to predict exactly when it will be ready. On top of this, you have built a world-class manufacturing capability, and you have confidence that the production ramp will be swift and steep.

Now imagine you are sitting in a program review just weeks before the product is scheduled to launch. The product development team is clearly scrambling, but they assure you the product will be ready as scheduled. Marketing says the timing is right. Manufacturing is gearing up. But then the engineering manager for a companion product speaks up and says that everything is going to have to push out a few weeks. The manager is responsible for a smaller peripheral product that is an integral part of the whole marketing package. And he just found out that *his* development team is "three to four weeks behind schedule."

This is essentially what happened in early 1993 when the full launch of the Intel Pentium® processor was delayed because an important peripheral product—the chipset—was not ready for production. The "three to four week delay" ended up being two full months. The chipset project, requiring roughly 38-person years, had impeded the success of a microprocessor project requiring closer to 500-person years. As you can imagine, the circumstances the chipset development team worked under during those two months gives new meaning to the term crunch time. And the attention they received from "on high" did not end when that chipset was finished. A message was sent and received that never again would a peripheral product hold up the launch of a new microprocessor family. Whatever needed to be fixed in that particular product division better get fixed!

Just an Anomaly?

A closer look at this division's performance (referred to from now on as PCD for Peripheral Components Division) revealed that this was not an isolated incident. PCD's chipset development projects had been slipping by an average of 40 percent from internally defined schedule end dates. For example, developing a chipset with a 15-month schedule was taking about 21 months. It was typical for PCD's product designs to be revised three or more times before being deemed ready for high volume production. (A typical revision adds at least a few weeks to the development time.) And it was common for one or two customers to find "bugs" that required another revision. Each of these measures provided an indication that PCD was struggling with its ultimate performance goal—*break-even time*. Break-even time is a measure of the time from first investigation of a new product to the time that product begins making a profit.[1]

Adding to the challenges of PCD, was the fact some of the most talented development engineers had decided they could find a more rewarding work environment elsewhere in the company. The leadership of PCD decided something needed to change. To their credit, one of the first things they did was to involve the "troops" in assessing the cause of current woes. Based on focus group feedback, a representative team identified three root causes of PCD's problems.

Self-Diagnosed Root Causes of Problems
1. Chronic Crunch Time

As microprocessor launches became more frequent, the time available for producing peripheral supporting products had shrunk accordingly. Engineers in PCD said that it had been okay when they spent six to eight weeks in crunch-time mode on previous project generations, because they usually had several months of normal work hours in between crunch times. But now, it seemed like crunch time never really ended. As soon as the design team passed off one design to the validation team, the next one was waiting for them, and already behind schedule.

2. Unreasonable Top-Down Schedules

Schedules were primarily based on top-down deadlines derived from analysis of optimal market timing for the product being developed. Although PCD had been consistently slipping these schedules, the end date for the next new product would often challenge the team with an even shorter schedule than last time. The team members considered the top-down end dates unreasonable, based on recent past performance.

3. Poor Communication Between Functional Teams

Each functional team complained that its "feeder" team was delivering subpar work. For example, the design team felt it was not getting what it expected in terms of architecture and requirements documentation. At the same time, the validation team accused the design team of providing chip models that were inadequate from a validation standpoint. It was common to hear one functional group accuse another of "throwing stuff over the wall," rather than conducting a coordinated passdown of agreed-to deliverables.

From the data collected in these focus group sessions, a rough picture was emerging of what it had been like to work in this division lately:

> Almost as soon as you finish one product, the next one is approaching crunch time. So you look for shortcuts. You worry about how they will affect the overall quality of the product, but you have little choice. Inevitably, you are quickly back to working overtime several nights a week. Some of the shortcuts come back to haunt you as rework and/or finger pointing from another functional team. More overtime. Meanwhile, the shortcuts taken on the previous-generation product are also haunting you. Customers are finding bugs, and each time they do, you hear about it.

No wonder people were starting to believe there had to be a better way and were looking outside PCD, or if need be, outside the company, to find it.

There Must Be a Better Way

PCD was committed to finding a better way. And by the time the next new microprocessor launch rolled around (the Intel Pentium Pro® processor), they had found a way to significantly improve on each of the break-even time indicators. Figure 1 compares PCD's performance before and after the identified root causes were addressed. The *before* performance is typical across several generations of chipset products; the *after* performance represents the Intel 440FX® chipset that supported the Pentium Pro® processor family.

Performance Indicators	PCD's Typical Performance Before	PCD's Performance After
Performance Against Top-down Deadlines	30-50% slip	10% slip
Performance Against Team Commit Date	Didn't have one	0 slip
Revisions Prior to High Volume Manufacturing	4	1
Bugs Discovered by the Customer	2	0

Figure 1. PCD's Performance Before and After Addressing Root Causes

The improved indicator performance resulted in the best break-even time in PCD history for this class of products. From a quality perspective, the team testing the design (the validation team) noticed the difference immediately. A key customer also noticed the difference when they saw the first samples of the 440FX® and transferred orders from the previous generation chipset. Even the trade magazines, which had been pretty rough on previous generations of chipsets, had nothing negative to say about the 440FX®. It went on to generate more revenue than any other nonmicroprocessor product at Intel (at least until that time), but there was another indicator that may be even more telling than those already described.

The 440FX® team was made up of many of the same engineers that had produced the product in previous generations. The timeframe given to develop it was similar to past ones, if not shorter. And when the project began, the team, as usual, felt it was already falling behind. When this successful project ended, focus groups were held again to understand what had changed. The most interesting thing to which the team members agreed was that on this project *there was almost no crunch time*. This team had met or beat each of its committed milestone dates. (The team's commitment throughout the project was 10 percent later than the top-down deadline.) When approaching a milestone, it was common for certain team members to work some long days and make sure they were going to keep their commitment. But that was it. For the most part, this team was working "regular" hours—regular for a high-tech engineering organization—a phenomenon that was not lost on its colleagues still doing projects the old way (more about this later).

What's Going On Here?

What began as somewhat of a black eye for PCD turned out to be a tremendous opportunity to understand the dynamics of complex project management in highly competitive environments. The interpretation (Figure 2) of what was going on, and how PCD overcame it, is based on observing the development of this one family of peripheral chipsets over four successive product generations. What was slowly revealed was a *vicious cycle* that could only lead to:

- earlier and earlier crunch time,

- mediocre if not poor project execution and

- difficulty retaining talented engineers.

The presence of this vicious cycle in environments characterized by highly competitive markets, and high complexity, has since been confirmed (anecdotally) by project leaders and team members in many different companies in several industries. What follows is a glimpse of life in the vicious cycle.

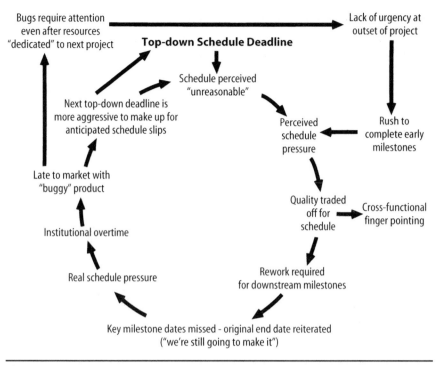

Figure 2. A Vicious Cycle

The Guarantee

In the electronics industry complex projects often begin with a defined end date. In a highly competitive environment, windows of market opportunity are relatively short, so a project is usually initiated with a guarantee from someone that it can be delivered on time. Project sponsors (upper management) often have an interesting way of getting this guarantee. If a selected project manager is unsure the date can be met, sponsors have been known to respond: "Then we'll find somebody that *is* sure the date can be met!" Through this tactic, sponsors have an excellent chance of getting the guarantee they are after. As a result, the first draft of the schedule is defined by a few "key players" working backwards from the guaranteed delivery date.

Another common phenomenon in pressurized environments is that projects are often slow in getting staffed. This is often, at least partly, because the pool of engineers that will be moving to this project are still responding to product issues from the last project. Responding to customer emergencies, and backfilling details that they had to leave out originally because they were so far behind, takes time. Resources are moved to the next project behind schedule, relative to the guaranteed delivery date that has already been established. This problem is only exacerbated when team members require training before they can become productive. It is common for project leaders not to panic when the project gets off to a bit of a slow start. After all, it's still early in the schedule and there is plenty of time to catch up.

Time's Up, I Guess I'm Done

But the team members can sense that something very familiar is happening. They are falling behind again. And if they fall behind, they soon will experience crunch time once more. When this occurs, the first tactic calls for team members (often a few of the most experienced) to push back on the draft schedule. Project leadership is often willing to extend some of the early task durations, as long as it does not affect the ultimate "guaranteed" delivery date. Pushing out the end date would be unacceptable.

Eventually, it becomes obvious that extending task duration on early milestones has pushed out the project end date. This is when crunch time becomes a real threat, and to avoid that, team members will begin to look for trade-off opportunities: "I'll never finish this task on time, but I have to say I'll be done next week, so I'll have to take some shortcuts. I'd prefer to do a higher quality job, but I have no choice." Because the schedule discussion to date has been almost exclusively about dates, with little or no attention to the quality of specific task outputs, trade-offs will always be in favor of saving time.

Institutionalized Crunch Time

Unfortunately, these trade-offs are not free. They are typically first noticed by the downstream team, which has to work with the outputs of the upstream teams. This leads to the finger pointing mentioned earlier and sometimes to rework. If the shortcuts go unnoticed at this time, it simply turns into rework later in the project when schedule pressure is even greater.

Sooner or later, the combination of a perceived unreasonable schedule, and the rework caused by trading off on quality, leads to institutionalized overtime (crunch time). PCD had an operational definition for this phenomenon—free pizzas are provided at work three or four nights a week, and team members are expected to stay at work through dinner time.

The "Acceptable" Lie

This is the part of the cycle that makes it truly vicious (self-reinforcing such that it feeds on itself and gets worse and worse). Although the team is getting further and further behind relative to a published schedule, they are telling each other (and upper management) that everything is okay. They do this because it is "unacceptable" to surface the possibility that the guaranteed date will be missed. In many cases, individuals have asked for guidance in setting some priorities, because intermediate goals are not going to be met. But they are told everything is a priority. One industry insider has pointed out that when managers refuse to set priorities, they become largely irrelevant as managers.

When team members realize they are not going to get guidance on priorities, they resign themselves to doing "the best they can" and to avoid becoming scapegoats. When the leader asks how it's going, they say "fine," or change the subject. Team leaders don't probe too deeply into these responses, because they really don't want to hear bad news. For these reasons, it appears to upper management as if everything is on track, until the end date or a key milestone is reached and the deliverable is not done. At this point, something, or someone, needs to be blamed for ruining a project that was "going perfectly well until just now." Engineers, who begin with the desire to work on the most critical and visible deliverables, quickly learn that the key to success is never to get caught in the position of being the ones blamed for "ruining a perfectly good project." They do this by complaining up front that the schedule is too aggressive, and then saying they are on track for their particular tasks. And if need be, they deliver whatever they have when the due date comes.

One team referred to the behaviors just described as "schedule chicken." Everyone is waiting for someone else to disclose that their part is really behind schedule. The longer this game goes on, the more likely it is that someone will get caught and become the scapegoat. But as long as you aren't the one who confesses or gets caught, it doesn't really matter that you are just as far behind your own schedule. You can imagine what happens to productivity as the tension builds leading up to the identification of a scapegoat.

Protecting the Customer
Upper management has its own problems in this pressure-cooker scenario. Telling key customers that a market window will be missed far in advance, is essentially like telling them they better go find a different supplier.

Experienced marketers know that if they keep the customer convinced until late in the game that the product will be ready on time, they stand a good chance of keeping the customer even if (when) the new product delivery slips a few weeks or even months. But no one likes to deliver bad news to the customer. Customer relations would be much easier if the project team would just figure out how to deliver on schedule. Upper management doesn't care how teams do it; they just want the product done on time. Because they remember that the last product came out a couple months late, they are inclined to ask for a guaranteed delivery prior to when the product is actually needed. In this way, when the project team comes in a couple months late, the customer may only be affected by a couple weeks.

You may have detected the dynamic that is evolving here between upper management and the team. Upper management sets overly aggressive goals in hopes of making up for the inevitable schedule slips. Team members always complain that the schedule is too tight, but never actually say it can't be done, because in the past they have been ignored or watched others get punished. So the perceived schedule pressure is more extreme and felt earlier by the project team on each successive project. Meanwhile, markets get more and more competitive, and upper management adds more and more pressure on each successive project. And every time it is finally revealed that the project delivery date is going to slip, even having taken many short-cuts, everyone acts as if this result is completely unexpected.

Somehow, the vicious cycle removes the integrity from schedule reporting and tracking, and the schedule essentially loses all meaning. In many cases, if there is not a dedicated resource for maintaining the schedule, it isn't even utilized below the milestone level after a couple months into the project. And if there are resources dedicated to keeping the schedule current, team members often view them as irrelevant, and find ways to minimize the impact of updating the schedule.

One could say that the vicious cycle reduces a team's *commitment* to a project schedule and goals. It turns out that the concept of commitment is crucial for reliable schedule performance, for awakening innovation and getting teams to strive for extraordinary performance (more on this in Chapter 9). This means commitment is also at the heart of escaping the vicious cycle, as was done by the 440FX® team. So how did they do it?

The First "Solution"

In 1993, as PCD was attempting to rebound from all the unwelcome and negative visibility, they did not have the benefit of standing back and viewing what we've just described as the vicious cycle. But they did have a list of defined root causes. After examining them, PCD decided to focus primarily on the issue of cross-functional communication by defining a standard process flow for chipset development. It was reasoned that if each functional subteam knew what to expect from each other, some of the finger pointing would stop, and the less experienced engineers would be able to contribute sooner. This should improve overall team productivity and speed up delivery.

The leadership of PCD also had some empathy in regard to the "unreasonable deadlines" root cause. In fact the vice president of the division had been quoted as saying, "The road to Hell is paved with projects that had to be done by Comdex." (Comdex was, at the time, the major computer trade show and the largest industry opportunity for marketing new products.) But recognizing this did not change the fact that there are hard and fast dates when products have to be ready in order to hit their targeted market window. The fact that windows were getting smaller and closing faster did not negate the fact that a missed window could translate into the loss of many millions of dollars in revenues throughout the life of the product. In some cases, this reality made it a bad business decision to invest in developing a product if the window couldn't be hit. Pushing out deadlines just was not going to be considered a viable solution.

It took a team of eight people, with representatives from each functional area, about three months to develop the division's new *process flow document*. It was arguably better than some of the past process flow documents, but this wasn't their first time down the process flow document path. The main body was only about 20 pages and focused on the major outputs of the development process rather than listing how specific tasks were to be done. The main document referenced a few "how-to" guides for aspects of development that had proven difficult in the past.

The document was made available electronically to the entire division about midway through the development of the next chipset—the one immediately following the product that delayed the Pentium® processor. Some of the subteam leaders for this project had participated on the process-flow team and they followed the guide closely. There is some evidence that these select subteams performed more efficiently than past baseline performance. However, the teams and individuals that had not participated in producing the process flow saw it as just another collection of somebody else's ideas. The performance in these other subteams was essentially unchanged and, therefore, the overall break-even time performance for this product was just slightly improved over the previous product. The process flow document was apparently not going to be enough to lead PCD out of its vicious cycle.

Stopping the Insanity

The chipset just completed was a product roadmap "filler." It did not support the next new microprocessor family but was designed to support Pentium® processor proliferations. Hence, it did not come under the same scrutiny as the previous one. However, the next chipset was the 440FX®, and it *was* slated to support the new Pentium Pro® processor launch—a new micro-processor product family. Believing in the old saying that it is insanity to do the same thing over and over and expect a different result, the 440FX® project manager (we'll call him Ted) decided to take a different approach. Although he was very attuned to the need to hit market windows, he sensed that the current approach of "simply refusing to hear that it can't be done" was not working.

Like all previous projects, by the time Ted was assigned as project manager and had a chance to staff the team, the project was already behind on the top-down defined milestone schedule. But Ted was completely committed to hearing what the project team thought was possible, and keeping the channels of communication open, even if he didn't like what he heard. He reasoned that if the project was not on track to meet the top-down required date, knowing it ahead of time would be better than discovering they weren't going to make it at the very end of the project. This way there might be an opportunity to recover, even if it meant making some tough trade-off deci-sions. Ted stuck to his commitment. Over the next 12 to 14 months (primarily during the design and validation phases of the project), he experienced both successes and frustrations that exceeded his wildest imagination. Below are a few of the lessons he learned.

Lesson 1: Estimates are not Promises
Given PCD's history of "don't-really-ask, don't-really-tell" project planning

and tracking, Ted knew he had to somehow distinguish this project from other ones. He heard that other product divisions had been "kicking off" projects by getting the entire team into a room to agree on a high level plan and to "approve" the guaranteed end date. Ted decided to have a kick-off meeting, but instead of getting approval for the top-down date, he told the team he wanted to know when they really thought this project would be finished. After the team had used a process to rapidly identify and clarify major project deliverables and dependencies he said, "I'm not interested in estimates and confidence levels, I want to know when you can *promise* to deliver each major deliverable."

Ted was apparently successful in getting this distinction across, because the team definitely did not tell him what he wanted to hear. Almost worse than telling him an unacceptable end date, they told him they couldn't give him an end date at all! They reminded him that the project was in "discovery mode" until the *architecture document* was frozen. If he was really interested in promises, all they could give him now was a completion date for the architecture document.

People are happy to throw around estimates without adequate data, but that's not the case with promises. To make promises, people need quality information and a sense of control (or a level of confidence teams working in the vicious cycle are never going to have).

Lesson 2: Participative Planning is an Iterative Process
Team members simply refused to promise completion dates for milestones further out in the schedule than they could effectively plan. Ted ended up convening a series of participative planning meetings over the course of the project. Each meeting yielded commitments for project deliverables further out on the project timeline. Finally, when the project was within six months of completion, the team committed to a project end date. Not having a team-commit date until later in the project made Ted very uncomfortable; however, the team completed every major deliverable on or before the date they had promised. It should also be noted that the original team promises (or *team commit dates*, as they came to be called) defined in the planning meetings were never quite aligned to the top-down guaranteed date. On average they represented a 10 percent slip from that date.

When the team can only make commitments for part of the plan, the rest of the plan is just an estimate. Effective planning requires revisiting those estimates and turning them into commitments (as the team acquires information and/or confidence). Therefore, a team's initial plan should be considered incomplete. Other than the portion where commitments have been made, it is a draft that needs to be revisited and refined (iterated) periodically throughout the project.

Lesson 3: Planning is about Sharing Assumptions

For example, when Ted said he would settle for a promised date for delivery of the architecture document, what he really got was a set of widely disparate promises from the different design subteams. One subteam said they could have their part ready in 4 weeks. Another team said it would take them 11 weeks. And there were three teams with dates in between.

Rather than try to make sense of this disparity at the end of what had been a long and mostly positive planning day, Ted said he would meet with the overall design team leader and each subteam on the following day to understand how they came up with their dates.

It turned out that the different dates were based on very different assumptions. Although there had been up-front discussion on what a good architecture document consisted of, assumptions about the appropriate level of detail still varied. The 11-week team was very concerned about the inexperienced engineers that would be turning *their* architecture into a coded model of the chip (*chip model*). They had assumed that the architecture document needed to be foolproof. To ensure that, they needed to do everything but code the model themselves in the architecture document. The 4-week team, on the other hand, was anxious to complete the architecture and get a larger pool of engineers involved in coding. They desired to begin other concurrent tasks once the overall architecture was approved, so they wanted approval as soon as possible.

By the end of the next day, the assumptions had been sorted out, and all the subteams had agreed to the latter strategy. The design team was committed to delivering the architecture document (with adequate but not comprehensive detail) in 5 weeks, which just happened to end the week before the year-end holiday.

Lesson 4: Good Managers Help Team Members Manage Themselves

When designing silicon chips it is common to organize subteams around portions (functional blocks) of the chip (see Figure 3). In the past, subteam leaders would define the subtasks required for each major deliverable, review them with the team and document them along with resource assumptions and task duration in the form of a Gantt chart (Figure 4) or an automated schedule. Once or twice a month, the entire design team would meet to review progress against the schedule. This is the point at which individuals and subteams had learned that the safe approach was to say that everything was on track. Chances were, even if the team was a little behind, other teams were at least as far behind, and there was no reason to risk being singled out.

This looked and felt like everyone thought project management should look and feel, but it didn't provide much useful information to either the

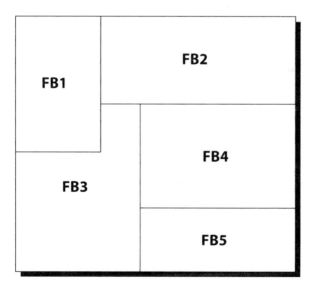

Figure 3. Silicon Chip Divided into Functional Blocks

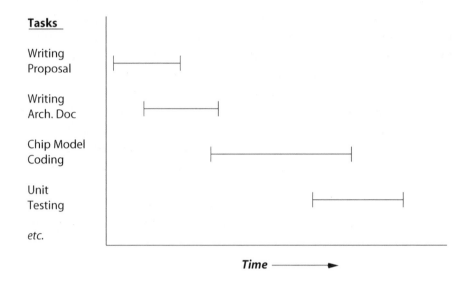

Figure 4. Gantt Chart Example

team members or the leadership of the project. With some coaching, the design team agreed to try another way. Instead of listing tasks, each subteam took its block and broke it into smaller portions (sub-blocks). Each sub-block had a unique label (see example below), and all the subtasks needed to be completed for that sub-block before it was considered complete. In this way, each subteam could identify ahead of time how many total sub-blocks they needed to complete and, therefore, how many sub-blocks per week they needed to complete on average (the "pace goal"). Now each team would know at the end of each week if they were really on track to meet the five-week completion date. Rather than discuss completion for a block in terms of percentages, each sub-block was simply *done* or *not done*.

With the sub-blocks defined, and a weekly pace goal understood, each individual on a subteam was asked to declare which sub-blocks they would complete that week. At the end of the week, each individual would report on their completed sub-blocks. A simple tracking sheet was used to track goals set and accomplished (see Figure 6). It was agreed that those who

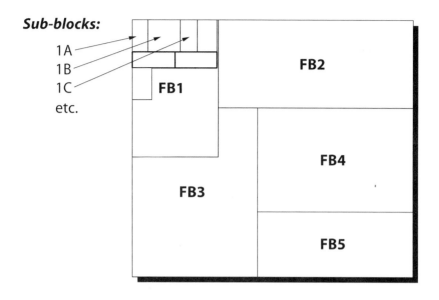

Figure 5. Breaking Functional Blocks into Sub-blocks

believed they were falling behind on their weekly goals would speak up immediately. (The end-of-week meetings were basically just opportunities to affirm that the team was on track.) When someone did speak up mid-week, it was the subteam leader's responsibility to find help within the team, or elevate the issue to the design team manager. Individuals were setting their personal goals and holding themselves accountable to meeting them, or asking for help. They were mostly managing themselves at the subteam level. With this self-management approach, all subteams and, hence, the overall team, were successful finishing the architecture document milestone on their committed date.

Lesson 5: Success is the Best Motivator

Remember that this team was coming off a string of not very satisfying projects. Recent past projects were likely perceived by many of the participants as a series of failures (missed milestones), leading up to an ultimate failure (missed project end date), followed by many reminders that short-cuts have their cost (rework and redesigns). You wouldn't expect that one small milestone success would have much impact on the team's perception

F.B.	Sub-block	Owner	Commit date	Done
1	1A	J.A.	Week 2	
	1B	J.A.	Week 2	
	1C	D.O.	Week 2	
	1D	C.F.	Week 2	
	etc.			
2	2A	T.E.	Week 2	

Figure 6. Subteam and Individual-Level Tracking

of itself, but it did. Actually, hitting a milestone date as scheduled (and promised) seemed to be a significant motivator for the team.

Having had their holiday vacations as planned—had the schedule slipped, many vacations would have been postponed—the team members came back anxious to take on the rest of the project. A second planning meeting was held and this time the team was willing to make firm commitments for the next three milestones—to the end of the design phase of the project. Their commitment came in about 10 percent beyond what top management had requested to complete this phase. This put Ted in a bit of an uncomfortable position, but the team members went on to either hit or exceed each milestone commitment. In the end, it looked like they just might finish the design phase when top management had requested. Ted suggested that the team pull in its commitment to that date. The team members were not amused with this suggestion. They reminded him that they had built in time at the end of the design phase for the inevitable "late bugs" that would have to be addressed. Ted hesitantly agreed to keep the commit date where it was, and the late bugs showed up as usual. As a result, the team members did not pull in their commitment as hoped, but they did complete the design phase when they promised they would.

There is a great deal of literature and debate about how to motivate people. Ted discovered that interim success is a very powerful motivator. Instead of trying to be a charismatic cheerleader, Ted had motivated the team by setting them up for success.

Lesson 6: Bottom-up AND Top-down

This may be the most important lesson of all. When the team came up with its date for completing the design phase, Ted published a memo to top management. The memo stated that the team understood the requested top-down date and would look for opportunities to achieve it, but it was committing to a different date, four weeks (about 10 percent) later than requested.

After the project was over, both Ted and the team members expressed that they disliked having two sets of dates for the project (top-down request and bottom-up commitment). It created top-down pressure for Ted much earlier than usual on the project. Even though Ted thought he was shielding the team from this pressure, they perceived that because he published both dates, he was still covertly holding them accountable to the top-down date.

From an outside perspective, having both dates seemed to be a key factor enabling Ted's team to get out of the vicious cycle. Judging by past history, if Ted would have published only the bottom-up commitment, management might have chosen someone else to lead the project—someone who could *guarantee* delivery on the top-down request date. However, PCD's performance history provides strong evidence that operating from only the top-down date would have led to typical schedule slips and quality problems. Although the team was not committed to the top-down request date, their awareness of the market window very possibly kept their commitments within a reasonable range of the deadline.

There seems to be some real value to having both market driven goals and a schedule the team uses to hold itself accountable to its own commitments. In the event that the bottom-up date is severely out of line with the top-down date, and no one can come up with a rational plan to close the gap, it is probably a prudent business decision to cancel or alter the project.

Making this decision before millions of dollars have been invested in trying to do the impossible would clearly be preferred to making it *after* wasting those dollars. Remember that in PCD they had been missing their market windows by a larger percentage (40 percent on average) when they only had a top-down date, and they never knew where they really stood until the project was supposed to be done.

Lesson 7: Slow Down to Go Faster

The largest impact on break-even-time performance on this project was *not* in speeding up the design, test or production phases of this product. The largest impact was realized by releasing the product to high volume production after just one design revision (instead of the typical three to five). There is nothing new here. This is the same lesson many manufacturing organizations learned in the 1980's with the Total Quality movement. However, it seems with all the pressure to keep up with the markets, businesses forgot how to slow down to go faster. By holding itself accountable to its own predefined indicators for deliverable and subdeliverable quality, this team saved itself two to three design revisions. The quality indicator discussion began in the planning meetings and continued between meetings as subteams and individuals set short-term goals and work priorities. Predictably, as communication about quality increased, the cross-functional finger pointing all but disappeared.

Lesson 8: Meeting Commitments is not Considered Heroic

As previously summarized, this team performed considerably better than all recent past PCD projects in terms of both execution and business success. It has also been mentioned that they did it without *institutionalized overtime* (crunch time). Team members worked extra hours at key points, primarily to make sure there was no chance of missing their own commitments. One would expect that the other teams in the division would be anxious to find out what this team was doing right. But that is not exactly what happened.

One of the things that sustains the vicious cycle is rewarding individuals and teams for being heroes—working super-long hours in order to *recover* from problems that shouldn't have ever occurred in the first place. Ted's team prevented the typical problems caused by shortcuts and burnout, so its performance did not look heroic at all. In fact, from the perspective of engineers working on vicious cycle projects, Ted's team looked like it was slacking off. Even PCD's top management did not initially recognize what Ted's team had accomplished. By the time the product was known to be a business success, the team members had long since moved to other projects, and the staff of PCD had changed dramatically, which is quite common in fast-moving companies.

As a result, it took PCD another product generation to learn the value of what Ted's team had accomplished. The chipset project immediately following fell back into many of the vicious cycle traps. The project team leadership focused more on the top-down request than on bottom-up input from the team to create the schedule. Predictably, the team missed its own schedule (although the team seemed to be caught by surprise when it did), the top-down request date was missed by more than 30 percent and quality was not equal to that of the previous generation. The lesson here is that individual project teams can use the methods described in this book to improve their own performance. But ultimately, if business managers (i.e., project sponsors) don't buy into the methods and change some of their own behaviors, the vicious cycle is likely to persist.

Nonetheless, the story does have a happy ending. When the 440FX® passed all other nonmicroprocessor products in revenue, the 440FX® team was finally recognized. An even more impressive recognition came a year later after PCD's project teams had lapsed back into the vicious cycle. When the time came to staff the next generation product (now three generations of chipsets after the Pentium® processor), top management didn't look for a project manager that would give them an unconditional guarantee; they went back to Ted. They decided that ultimately it was better to know what was really going on than to "hear what they wanted to hear."

Beyond Product Development
Chips, Chunnels and Other Complex Beasts
Unfortunately, in the computer industry, the vicious cycle is not limited to product development. It is triggered by complexity, which creates uncertainty, and competition, which we allow to create pressure. In consumer products industries, pressure comes from the desire to get better products to market before the competition. In many other industries, pressure comes from the practice of competitive bidding. Multiple organizations bidding

for the same work, without knowing what the other organizations are going to promise, ensures that everyone will make as aggressive a bid as they think they can (not necessarily one they believe they can deliver on). An example of a complex project planned and executed in this kind of competitive bidding environment is the Chunnel Project.

The Chunnel Project connected France and Britain by way of an underground tunnel beneath the English Channel, which can be accessed by train and automobile. The multi-billion dollar Chunnel opened a year late, cost about twice what the contractors bid for the job,[2,3] and the teams that began tunneling from each end didn't quite meet in the middle.[4] Although the construction schedule only slipped about 15 percent, the project leadership insisted it was not slipping at all until nine months before the end of the seven- year project—indicating unreliable data was being reported to management. There was also significant rework, including about $40 million in piping redesign alone.[5] This is not to belittle the challenges of such a project or the people who take them on. The Chunnel project was technically complex (not to mention dangerous), overseen by two different countries and numerous banks, planned under the pressure of competitive bidding and executed with the pressure of the whole world watching. Yet projects with similar pressure and complexity have been performed with excellent success.

The United States military has been developing leading-edge weapons systems for decades in the competitive bidding environment. And although it is common to hear horror stories about these projects' costs and schedule overruns, not all are poorly executed. One of the best success stories is the U. S. Navy's Polaris missile submarine program of the 1950's and 1960's, in which the first Polaris submarine was deployed three years before originally scheduled. Although it spanned 12 years and involved over 2,000 contractors, the Polaris program came within 2 percent of meeting its original cost estimate.[6] Unfortunately, success stories like Polaris are the exception and not the rule. There are myriad ways for complex projects to fail, but poor execution due to the vicious cycle is common and may be the most insidious. Even complex projects considered successful have not, in many cases, escaped the vicious cycle.

The Titanic Syndrome: Business Success does not Equal Execution Success
Producing a blockbuster movie is an extremely complex project in an industry with intense competition. The movie *Titanic* has grossed $1.8 billion, so far,

with a development cost of $200 million.[7] Because *Titanic* was inarguably a tremendous business success, director/producer James Cameron must be an exemplary project manager. Or is he? Cameron missed his planned release date by 6 months and overspent his budget by 100 percent (the original budget was $100 million). And the actors and crew complained that much of the filming occurred in a sweatshop-like atmosphere.[8] Luckily, Cameron works in an industry that is considered an art form, so no doubt there are still big-time investors willing to gamble that he will produce another master-piece. Of course in industries that are strictly business, this type of logic would never fly. Or would it?

Just as there are myriad things that can go wrong, there are some key things, which if done well, can make a poorly run project look great. Organizations that have developed a business advantage, for example, through exceptional marketing and/or manufacturing, can sometimes score big (like Cameron's *Titanic*) *in spite of* poor performance against project plans. Organizations with these "cash cow" projects are inclined to not want to change anything—"Sure it's not perfect, but what we're doing is working and the stakes are too high to risk any drastic changes." Project managers and leaders who are rewarded for using vicious cycle tactics will continue to propagate the vicious cycle even when project after project performs unreliably—at least until the business advantage goes away.

But there are potentially serious downsides to using business success as the only criteria to evaluate current project management practices. First of all, a poorly executed project that returned its investment four times, might have returned it four and a half or five times instead. In many industries this impact would be measured in millions, if not tens of millions, of dollars. Secondly, what is working financially may not be working in terms of human resources. In the hi-tech industry, talented knowledgeable workers are drawn to the leading edge of technology. But, as PCD found out, the most talented have the most choices. They will not work in the vicious cycle indefinitely. Finally, the third and maybe largest potential impact of letting vicious cycle projects persist is their impact on the larger organization.

Beyond the Individual Project

Although it is sometimes hard to convince project teams of it, projects are not carried out in a vacuum. Project-oriented organizations typically have many projects in progress at the same time and, overtly or covertly, all of those projects are vying for the same pool of limited organizational resources. Managing these organizations involves managing the project list (or sometimes the product or project roadmap) and making cross-project decisions. Cross-project decisions are decisions about how the limited available resources can best be utilized to achieve the business goals. They manifest themselves as decisions to start a new project, continue or stop current projects and/or reconfigure the mix of resources between existing projects. The simplified vicious cycle diagram (Figure 7) helps demonstrate how projects operating in the vicious cycle impact cross-project decisions.

This diagram focuses on how project performance data becomes unreliable and the impact the bad data has on current and future projects. Figure 8 reveals the larger impact of unreliable performance data. The "acceptable lies" induced and reinforced by the project's vicious cycle spur a complementary cross-project cycle that comes back to haunt each individual project.

Sometimes when a project is severely out of synch with the project plan (i.e., behind schedule, over budget, overextended with risks), the best thing

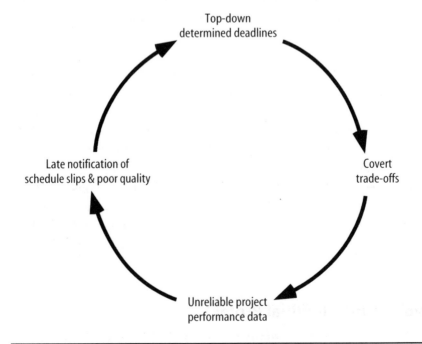

Figure 7. Simplified Project Vicious Cycle

for the organization would be to scrap the project and utilize the resources to better support the organization's business goals. However, when management does not have reliable project performance data, these decisions are made poorly or not at all. Evidence that an organization is not making these decisions is represented by the "unmanageable project list." Such lists instigate an ongoing effort to juggle 30 to 40 or even 100 projects when the organization is resourced to execute closer to 10 to 15 projects really well. Project teams operating in this environment (along with the aforementioned complexity and pressure) are much more likely to succumb to the project-level vicious cycle, which feeds the cross-project vicious cycle, which exacerbates the project-level vicious cycle, which . . . you get the idea.

Adding Complexity to Complexity
Cross-project Dependencies
As if managing an isolated complex project in a competitive environment isn't enough for the project manager, the lines between complex projects blur in many organizations. This occurs partly because of the resource sharing just described, but also because of the general movement towards

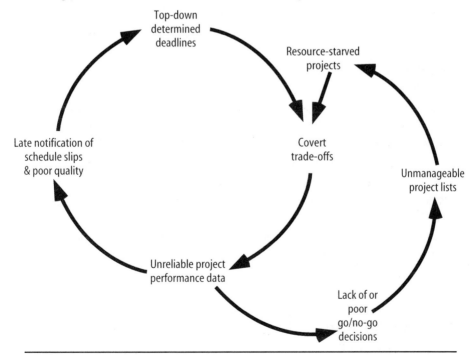

Figure 8. Cross-Project Vicious Cycle

integration of technology. In the high-tech industry, concurrency of development and integration of platforms and technologies often results in a complex network of dependencies between projects.

For example, companies that supply computer chips to computer manufacturers want to have as large a share of the total silicon in each computer as possible. One way to accomplish this is to offer a huge variety of combinations of semiconductor components to each manufacturer. The result is a domino effect. If the project to design one component falls into the vicious cycle, projects to produce other components and combinations of components are affected. Referring back to the case study, the only reason PCD's vicious cycle became more visible than many other projects in the company was because that particular chipset had an impact on the critical path of an even more strategic project.

This same complexity of scope is also present in competitive bidding environments. A physical-plant construction project may be sandwiched in between projects to develop a piece of real estate and to fit the plant with manufacturing equipment. These projects become interrelated with different individual projects needing to take on overall leadership at different times. Changes to the scope of any one of the projects have an impact on each of the others.

Supplier Management

Supplier management is a special complexity of scope case caused by interdependent projects. Suppliers are usually completely separate companies that have been contracted to provide an integral component of the project (either a product or a service). A supplier that performs reliably actually reduces the complexity of the overall project a little bit for the project leadership. However, a supplier that operates in the vicious-cycle mode can potentially destroy the overall project, and project managers are expected to account for this possibility. Larger projects may have suppliers who are dependent on other suppliers, etc. Today's project managers are often really managing a program of related projects, and each level of management above and below is dealing with more complexity than ever.

From the Vicious Cycle to a Benevolent One?

The picture painted so far has been rather grim. The vicious cycle feeds off complexity and competitiveness which, if anything, continue to grow in our work environments. As demonstrated in the case study, a dynamic that encourages managers and performers to work at cross-purposes with each other seems to inevitably build momentum. This momentum continues until there is a drastic change in the way individual projects and the overall organization are managed (or the organization implodes).

A more optimistic view might be to ask: What if the same dynamic momentum that creates the vicious cycle could be channeled into another kind of cycle? What if that cycle were a benevolent one, where crunch time is used sparingly, and performance gets progressively better, surpassing the levels that top management would even think of asking for based on past performance? This book concludes with a discussion about this benevolent cycle.

But even approaching the benevolent cycle requires first emerging from the vicious cycle. Hence, the focus of this book is in how to emerge from and stay out of both levels of vicious cycle (or to avoid them altogether if you are part of a new organization). The next chapter provides a framework intended to simplify how we think about project management in today's complex world. Part II will describe a commitment-based approach for managing individual complex projects in competitive environments. The process has been much refined, and some useful tools have been added, since Ted and his 440FX® team first used it to navigate out of the project vicious cycle in 1994. Additional guidance for applying this approach is provided in the appendix in the form of templates and checklists.

Part III deals with the cross-project vicious cycle and supplier management. These are often the domain of program managers (who manage across multiple projects), as well as managers responsible for a product line or a business division. There is a great deal of leverage at this level of management for preventing individual project managers from sliding into the project vicious cycle. Also provided is advice for adapting commitment-based project management for supplier management, and an explanation of the conditions that must be in place for it to be effective.

For those interested in management theory, Part IV hypothesizes about why the methods and tools described in this book work. It provides some insight into the origins of this particular mix of theory and practice. And it also explains how commitment management not only gets you out of the vicious cycle but can also lead to a benevolent cycle that ultimately produces not just reliable, but extraordinary, performance.

Summary

- Complex projects in a competitive environment are likely to fall into a *project vicious cycle*—a dynamic that evolves between management and the performers and inevitably leads to deception and poor performance.

- The project vicious cycle has a measurable negative impact on profitability, measured by:

  — time to break even in product development environments or

  — the ability to win future contracts in competitive bidding environments.

- Early indicators of the project vicious cycle are:

  — schedule slips of 30-50 percent or more,

  — amount of rework or revisions required,

  — cross-functional finger pointing (over the wall syndrome) and

  — institutional overtime (crunch time).

- Allowing individual projects (or even outside suppliers) to operate in the vicious cycle has implications well beyond individual projects. The project vicious cycle expands into the *cross-project vicious cycle.*

- Early indicators of the cross-project vicious cycle are:

— unmanageable project lists,

— poor go/no go decisions (projects operating outside of the project plan linger) and

— all projects, even the most strategic ones, complaining of being resource-starved.

■ This book provides a management approach called commitment-based project management along with templates and checklists for getting out of the vicious cycle. When practiced systematically at both the project and organization level, this method not only releases your organization from the vicious cycle, but is also the first step towards a benevolent cycle of excellent performance.

1. Charles H. House and Raymond L. Price, "The Return Map: Tracking Product Teams," *Harvard Business Review* (January-February 1991): 92-100.

2. George Dewan, "New Wonder: The Chunnel Tunnel Links Britain, France," *Newsday*, 5 May 1994, A20.

3. Shawn Tully, "Europe: Full Throttle Toward a New Era," *Fortune*, 20 November 1989, 131.

4. Drew Fetherston, *The Chunnel: Amazing Story of the Undersea Crossing of the English Channel* (New York: Random House, Inc., 1997).

5. Ibid.

6. H. M. Sapolsky, *The Polaris System Development: Bureaucratic and Programmatic Success in Government* (Cambridge: Harvard University Press, 1972).

7. Claudia Eller, "Studios Still Fighting the Battle of the Bulging Budget," *Los Angeles Times*, 13 January 1998, Home edition, Business section.

8. Patrick Goldstein, "View from 'Titanic': Oscars on Horizon, Profit Hard to See," *Los Angeles Times*, 16 December 1997, Home edition, Calendar section.

Combating Complexity
with Simplicity

There is no dearth of literature on project management. However, there is a relatively small and consistent set of themes that emerge in the vast majority of it: assembling and structuring the team, work-breakdown structure, estimating and scheduling, trade-off management, risk management, and getting the most out of human resources. Each of these topics has many subtopics, and everyone who writes or teaches about them has their favorite emphases and advice. But the fact that the vicious cycle and its symptoms (slipped schedules, rework, crunch time) are so widespread is evidence that project managers are having difficulty applying the myriad practices, principles and platitudes to their increasingly complex environments. It is apparently difficult to translate all this project management information into an approach that yields reliable and high quality project performance.

Sometimes the best way to combat complexity is with simplicity. What seems to be missing is an approach that takes into account how complex things have become and how fast things are moving in today's work environment. What is being proposed here is a simple framework for project management where a few rules can be applied at multiple levels. The framework is implemented through a network of regular meetings and management documentation that can potentially be limited to a few matrices and graphs. This is not so much a departure from the well-known topics listed above, as a new way of simplifying and organizing that information so that it can be used effectively to manage projects, project lists and even outside suppliers. To that end, this chapter will be a brief introduction to the methodology laid out in Part II.

Simple Framework: The Performance System Structure

From Rolls to Goals

The basis of this framework is not new. In fact, its roots are quite ancient. Performance System Structures derive from the time-tested practice of comparing actual amounts of something against the government rolls. The Latin term *contrarotulus*—against the rolls—is a root of our word *control.*[1,2] In today's organizations and projects, the rolls have been replaced with *the goals.* In order to remain in control, projects need to frequently compare

Figure 9. The Performance System Structure

actual performance against the goals and the plans to achieve those goals. **The performance system structure is the necessary structure for project feedback and control.** A simple model of the structure (Figure 9) is shown at left.

This structure needs to operate at each level of the organization. Just as organizations need regular data about how the entire organization is performing against its plans, project teams need more specific data about how the team is performing. Project subteams need even more specific information about their own performance and, finally, each individual team member needs data about how he or she is performing. Each level of the organization needs its own performance system and, of course, each performance system needs to align with the organization's overall business plans.

The Purpose of Reviewing Progress
Again, the performance system structure is not a major departure from conventional management wisdom. Most organizations and projects are already doing a fair amount of planning, tracking and reviewing. However, as complexity and competition have increased, many seem to have forgotten the purpose of planning, tracking and reviewing. **An effective performance system tells the project team (not just management) if everything is okay, or if the status quo needs to change in order for project goals to be attained.** In other words, performance systems enable project teams to make effective decisions throughout the life of a project. The key word here is *effective*. To be effective, the performance systems must provide decision makers with timely and accurate information about actual performance. To the extent that current approaches to planning, tracking and review are not accomplishing this, the team is not operating within the simple yet critical framework of the performance system structure.

Before describing how to ensure that a team makes effective decisions using timely and accurate information, it might be useful to describe an approach to planning and progress review that would best prevent it:

How to Prevent Timely and Accurate Performance Data

- Insist that project planning be done by a select few.

- Systematically review progress only at the overall project level.

- Review progress infrequently (once a month or less).

- Focus reviews on "what's going on" rather than on "actual performance against plans".

- Punish people for revealing bad news about actual performance.

If any of these behaviors sound familiar, your organization or team may need a simple way to improve your performance systems and, hence, your decision making.

Behaviors to Ensure Timely Decisions
Performance systems need to be in place at each organizational level of a project (e.g. overall project level, functional subteam level, and individual level), because decisions are made at each of those levels. Once the scope of a decision goes beyond how an individual is going to achieve his or her specific task goals, the decision needs to be visible to other affected team members. There needs to be a meeting.

The deeper project teams get into the vicious cycle, the more review meetings are reviled. Team members begin mumbling to themselves, "Why spend more time reviewing how behind we are, especially when we could be using the time to catch up?" Paradoxically, to avoid the vicious cycle, more frequent review meetings are needed. However, it is imperative that those meetings are run specifically to ensure good decision making based on timely and accurate performance data. The specifics for running these meetings will be provided later; the point here is that regular progress review meetings can and should be used to ensure that the team is operating with effective performance systems at each level. Table 10 summarizes the level and frequency of meetings recommended for staying in the performance system structure and enabling excellent decision making throughout the project.

Meeting Name	Meeting Purpose	Attendees	Frequency	Timing
Team Planning Meeting	Establish a commitment-based plan	All contributors to the project (not necessarily all at same time)	Roughly every three months (more frequently in beginning)	Begin when definition is reasonably clear and project 25-50% staffed
Project-Level Progress Review	Manage commitments *across* functions (subteams)	Subteam leaders and anyone else who owns upcoming deliverables	Once a week on average—no less than twice a month	Regular scheduled time—usually beginning of week
Subteam-Level Progress Review	Manage commitments *within* functions (subteams)	All members of the subteam	At least once a week	Just before the project-level progress review

Table 10. Managing the Project with Regular Meetings

The first row in the table represents planning meetings. These ensure that each team member understands the overall plan, as well as his or her specific role, with great clarity. The next two rows represent progress review meetings at the project-team and then the subteam levels. Overall project performance needs to be reviewed at a minimum of twice a month, and at least weekly during high decision-making periods. Subteams should be meeting at least weekly whenever they are actively contributing to the project. Note that subteams meet just prior to project level meetings to ensure that the performance data presented at the project level is fresh and accurate. Each individual member of the team needs to review his or her own performance several times a week, so that early warning can be provided if there is any jeopardy of impeding subteam progress.

You might be wondering how anything could possibly get done in the presence of all these meetings. Try to suspend that concern for now. Chapters 5 and 6 provide specific advice for keeping meetings brief and productive. The typical team member should spend 15 to 30 minutes per week in meetings designed to track and coordinate the work (not counting the periodic whole-team meetings). Subteam leaders will spend more time coordinating work in meetings because they are the link between individual performance and project performance, and that is a critical part of the value they bring to the project team. It is the subteam leader's job to ensure that each individual is working in the performance system structure. Surfacing issues in real time, and getting decisions made, is time very well spent, as long as the decisions are driven by accurate performance data.

Simple Rules: Commitment Management

The Performance Data Game

Teams operating in the vicious cycle are playing a game. It is not a game that can be won, but it is a game that can be survived. Recall that most members of a team in the vicious cycle perceive the project plan as unreasonable. This belief is then further reinforced at each stage in the vicious cycle. When being held accountable for a task perceived as impossible, a reasonable strategy is to not let anyone know how you are performing. When no one knows how you are performing, you won't get much praise, but you may avoid punishment.

In contrast, a person who is personally committed to a goal will want to know at all times exactly how he or she is performing. Accurate performance data defines the gap that needs to be closed in order to succeed. A concert pianist trying to perfect her performance would never wear earplugs while practicing. This same principle applies to projects. When the people doing the work are committed to the plan (and the planning and reporting process), it is in their best interests to be very honest about current performance. Hence, accurate project performance data depends on team commitment to the project plan.

Measuring Commitment

Commitment is often viewed as rather intangible and unmeasurable. As with the concept of motivation, managers tend to stay away from commitment because it is just too vague. But that doesn't have to be the case, if we define it in operational terms. **For our purposes, a commitment is a personal promise to finish a specific deliverable at a certain time and to predefined quality criteria.** Promises are very different from the goals and estimates that make up the plans of teams struggling in the vicious cycle. People and organizations fall short of goals all the time. In fact, in some organizations, any individual or team that consistently hits defined goals is accused of sandbagging—purposely setting unchallenging goals.

Estimates are also not expected to be binding. An estimate is a best guess. Sometimes estimates are based on data and many times they are not. In either case, estimates are expected to have a margin of error, which often creates discussions about "confidence levels" that move us even further away from commitment. Personal promises, at least as defined here, are a matter of honor. As long as some simple rules are followed at all levels of the project, team members will stay committed to the project plan, and decisions will be made with accurate performance data. These rules break out into planning rules and reporting rules.

Planning Rule #1: *Plans are stated in terms of who is delivering what to whom and when (deliverables versus tasks).* Everyone needs to be very clear about what commitments have been made. Commitments shouldn't be about behaviors (working hard or using defined tools and methods); they should be about completing valued portions of the project (deliverables). It is easier to get clear about deliverables than about tasks and behaviors.

Planning Rule #2: *Quality requirements are predefined for each deliverable before dates are committed.* If rework is to be avoided, deliverables must meet the overall project needs the first time around. Effective project plans clarify the required quality of each deliverable.

Planning Rule #3: *Whoever will execute the plan needs to participate in developing the plan.* This is strongly recommended to establish commitment in the first place. It is possible to get people committed to someone else's plan, but it is a lot easier to let the commitment build as the team builds its own plan.

Reporting Rule #1: *Performance data simply shows whether what was committed to be done is done or not.* In vicious cycle projects, the plan is not stated clearly enough to report progress this way. Instead, team leaders estimate the percentage of a given task that is completed. Unfortunately, when this method is used, the last 10 percent of a task usually takes about as long as the first 90 percent. Focusing on deliverables versus tasks will make it unnecessary to estimate percentages. Individuals will report what they finished this week, which can be rolled up to what the subteam finished this week, which can be summarized into what the whole project team has accomplished so far.

Reporting Rule #2: *Whoever executes the plan generates the performance data that is used to make decisions.* Because the most critical performance data constitutes actual performance (what's done) against the committed plan (what's supposed to be done), it should be simple to track and report. Individuals should report out to their subteams, and subteam leaders should report out at the overall project level. Individual performers are closest to the work and the related issues, so when the data suggest a decision needs to be made, the performers should make the first recommendation. Subteam leaders will need to roll data up for examination at the next level of the project, but this should not involve complex analyses that potentially filter what is really going on. If it is requiring dedicated resources to report project performance, it is probably being made more difficult than need be.

Reporting Rule #3: *Expect early warning of commitments that may be missed and never punish anyone for providing early warning.* This is probably the single most important rule, and the hardest rule to follow, for teams that have been operating in the vicious cycle. When it is being followed, no one ever reports that a deliverable will be late on the same day it is due. As soon as the individual or subteam believes a commitment is in jeopardy, the concern (and a recommendation) is raised up to the next level. The heart of the vicious cycle is the failure to surface issues and make timely and sound decisions.

Commitment Management

When the above rules are followed, the project plan becomes a network of personal commitments, and day-to-day project management becomes "commitment management"—a systematic process of making and meeting commitments. When commitments are managed at short intervals through the meetings previously described, milestones are almost always hit and crunch time becomes an occasional choice on the part of team members. When commitments are being managed effectively, trade-offs are always out in the open. They occur frequently, they are expected and they are viewed as opportunities to keep the project on track. It looks and feels very different from the vicious cycle where the only trade-off decisions that make it to daylight are the large nasty ones.

Simple Documentation:
The Deliverables Matrix and the PAC Chart

So what does a commitment-based project plan look like? It looks pretty simple. The primary documentation is called a deliverables matrix. The matrix is the output of the initial planning process and provides the structure for regular project-level review meetings. Consistent with the simple rules for planning, it defines the owner and key users of each deliverable. It also has a column to document if the owner and users for each deliverable have gotten clear about the required quality of each deliverable. It contains the date when the owner has committed to finish the deliverable and the status of the deliverable—done or not done.

The actual commit dates for each deliverable are often not all filled in at the beginning of the project. When you are documenting commitments instead of estimates, team members may not be willing to provide dates for

Deliverables	Owner	User(s)	Quality Reqs	Commit Date	Done?
Project Plan	Jake	Debra, Lee, Bill, Jenifer	Y	WW10	
Architecture Doc.	Debra	Bill Jenifer	Y	WW13	
Product Specification	Debra	Bill, Jenifer	Y	WW15	
Demand Schedule	Lee	Jake	Y	WW15	
1st Prototype	Bill	Jenifer	N	WW18	
Test Plan	Jenifer	Bill	Y	WW17	

Figure 11. Example of a Partial Deliverables Matrix

F.B.	Sub-block	Owner	Commit date	Done
1	1A	J.A.	Week 2	
	1B	J.A.	Week 2	
	1C	D.O.	Week 2	
	1D	C.F.	Week 2	
	etc.	.		
2	2A	T.E.	Week 2	

Figure 12. Subteam and Individual-Level Tracking

later deliverables at the outset of the project. This is an important and subtle element of the commitment management approach that will be discussed in detail in Chapters 5 and 7. For now, remember that in the chipset case study, Ted's team reduced schedule slippage to the top-down requested date 30 to 50 percent when Ted stopped "committing the team" to that date at the outset of projects.

Often an even simpler chart of some sort will be used at the subteam and individual levels within and between the weekly subteam meetings. Figure 12 is an example from the case study in Chapter 1. Recall that the design team broke functional blocks of the chip into sub-blocks to identify deliverables that one engineer could produce in a week or less. Several more examples of individual and subteam level tracking sheets are provided and discussed in Chapter 6.

The Performance Against Commitment (PAC) Chart
The deliverables matrix and the subteam tracking chart define what needs

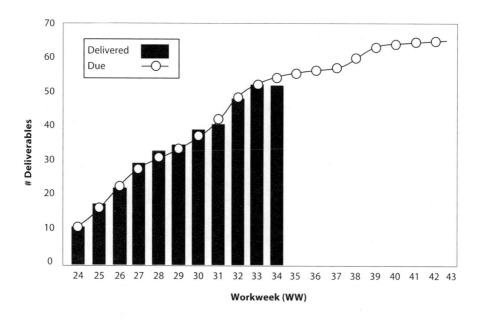

Figure 13. The Performance Against Commitment (PAC) Chart

to be talked about in the regular progress review meetings at each perspective level. Throughout the project, there should always be a simple visual indicator of how the overall project is doing. Consistent with the framework at the beginning of this chapter, the indicator should compare something actual to something planned. Because we are tracking commitments, the best overall indicator for the project is commitments met against commitments made. For teams basing their project reviews on the deliverables matrix, this indicator will essentially update itself at each meeting. This is the indicator that both the project manager and the manager at the next level up should be most concerned about, because **past performance is the only reliable predictor of future performance.**[3]

If a gap starts to develop between the bars (representing cumulative commitments met) and the line (representing cumulative commitments made), the team is falling behind. Experience shows that any team that misses more than 5 or 10 percent of its commitments and expects to finish the project on time (without some other trade-off) is probably fooling itself. When this is the case, it is important that senior managers understand Reporting Rule #3 (never punish an early warning). The PAC chart is an extremely valuable indicator and tool for making cross-project decisions (as well as monitoring outside suppliers). But it only works until teams are punished for publishing what's really going on. At that point, commitment will erode, and the vicious cycle will return. This is discussed from the perspective of business managers (project sponsors) in Chapter 7.

The PAC chart and the deliverables matrix are not the only documentation recommended, but they are at the center of the commitment management method and give you an idea of how simple effective project management documentation can be. Figure 14 identifies a few more types of documentation that will also be addressed in the book. Each type of documentation is referenced to the meeting where it is used.

Meeting Name	Meeting Purpose	Documentation Used
Cross-Project Review Meeting	Manage the project list	PAC Chart Milestone chart
Project-Level Progress Review	Manage commitments *across* functions (subteams)	Deliverables Matrix Risk Matrix PAC Chart Early-Warning Reports
Subteam-Level Progress Review	Manage commitments *within* functions (subteams)	Subteam tracking tool (on paper or wall display) Individual tracking tools

Figure 14. Reporting Documents and Meetings Where They are Used

A Word about Project Management Software

You will notice that although this book provides step-by-step advice, it does not include advice on choosing or using specific automated scheduling tools. There are two reasons for this. One is that there is already an abundance of advice about this at bookstores and software outlets, and it didn't seem necessary to try and reproduce that here. The other reason is that scheduling software is often viewed as *the* tool for effective management of projects. Sophisticated scheduling software does make it easier to run alternative scenarios when things change (e.g. when teams are falling behind). However, those scenarios are only as good as the information that is fed into them (which is often not very good for a variety of reasons). And, if the real goal is to stay on schedule throughout a project, then putting lots of effort into maintaining a system designed to deal with recovery seems to send the wrong message. When teams are working in a commitment framework, *and* the members themselves see value in maintaining an automated schedule for their own use, they should by all means do so. Automated tools are also helpful for teams that are truly accountable for a project budget, but this is probably the exception rather than the norm in many industries.

This chapter has provided an overview of how to manage complex projects based on a simple framework, a network of regular meetings, a few rules and simple documentation. Part II is organized around the planning and review meetings and describes in detail the steps to implementing commitment management and escaping (or better yet avoiding) the vicious cycle.

Summary

- Today's project managers and business managers need a simpler project management framework and approach.

- Project teams need frequent, well-run meetings at each level to make timely decisions based on actual performance relative to the project plan.

- Sound decisions are based on timely and accurate performance data. The vicious cycle erodes team commitment to project plans and makes it threatening to report accurate performance data.

- A commitment is a personal promise to finish a specific deliverable (or subdeliverable) at a certain time, to predefined quality criteria.

- Follow these three rules to develop a commitment-based plan:

  1 Plans are stated in terms of who is delivering what to whom and when (deliverables versus tasks).

  2 Quality requirements are predefined for each deliverable before dates are committed.

  3 Whoever will execute the plan needs to participate in developing the plan.

- Follow these three rules to report on and manage commitments effectively throughout the project:

  1 Performance data should simply show whether what was committed to be done is done or not.

  2 Whoever executes the plan generates the performance data that is used to make decisions.

  3 Expect early warning of commitments that may be missed and never punish anyone for providing early warning.

- Documenting progress against a commitment-based plan can and should be relatively simple. It is recommended that all documentation be anchored to the deliverables matrix and PAC chart.

1. James R. Beniger, *The Control Revolution: Technological and Economic Origins of the Information Society* (Cambridge: Harvard University Press, 1986).

2. *The American Heritage Dictionary of the English Language* (New York: American Heritage Publishing Co., 1969).

3. Thomas F. Gilbert, *Human Competence: Engineering Worthy Performance*, Tribute Edition (Washington DC: The International Society of Performance Improvement, 1996).

PART II

Managing Commitments
with Meetings

The Commitment-Based Project Plan

In 1994, just about the time Ted and his team were beginning to apply the method that would lead them out of the vicious cycle, a production supervisor in a wafer fabrication plant was also discovering the power of performance systems. Dub was already a successful supervisor, but he had been to some training on individual performance systems and decided to give it a try. To his amazement, his already successful team increased productivity (number of wafers properly processed) almost 20 percent *the first week* he implemented a performance system. The system consisted mostly of a pace goal (wafer output per person, per day) and individual self-tracking sheets so that each person knew if he or she was on pace at all times.

The jump in productivity seemed so effortless to Dub that he told the team the goal for the next week would increase 15 percent over what they had just accomplished. At the end of that next week Dub was even more amazed. Productivity had dropped to just below the original level. Dub was learning an extremely important management lesson, and he was bright enough to understand what it was. The people doing the work need to have some input about their own performance goals.

At the beginning of the next week, Dub told the team members he was having some trouble forecasting their output, and he would like their help in doing so. He also reminded them that because of equipment limitations, their operation was historically the "bottleneck" of the production line. So any increase in productivity could have a direct impact on overall factory output. Within a couple weeks, the team had reset their own run rate at 120 percent of their baseline productivity. From that point forward, Dub encouraged the team to "aim higher" when the data suggested they could be even more productive, but the decision to alter the pace goal was always made jointly with the team. Several months later Dub's team was reliably operating at 155 percent of the original baseline, and he was asked to begin managing a larger portion of the factory.

Another way of framing the lesson Dub learned is that you cannot make commitments for other people. To commit to performance goals, performers need to participate in the planning process. For a small team of individual performers doing an ongoing task (like production), the planning process can be a short weekly meeting. For complex projects, the planning process is considerably more involved. However, it is quite possible to carry out this process *with* participation of all team members *and* do it very rapidly. Chapter 4 will describe a meeting structure for developing a commitment-based plan rapidly and with full team participation. However, planning rapidly is not accomplished by taking shortcuts. This chapter recommends key planning components, and a sequence for addressing them, regardless of who develops the plan.

The document that summarizes a commitment-based plan is a deliverables matrix. The planning components that must be understood in order to develop the deliverables matrix are the project's:

- ultimate deliverable,

- customer(s),

- high-level measures of success,

- customer deliverables,

- internal deliverables,

- deliverables map,

- internal-deliverable quality criteria and

- first-horizon commits.

Although the vicious cycle is more likely and more wicked on very complex projects, the planning approach described here has been demonstrated to add value for less complex, and even, simple projects. Because complex projects tend to involve lots of specialized technology and terminology, wherever possible, simpler projects will also be used to demonstrate specific aspects of the approach. Also, examples will consistently refer to three levels of project organization (project level, subteam level and individual level). The approach being described is easily adapted for two levels of organization and is currently being used successfully on projects with at least four—project level, subteam level, sub-subteam level and individual level.

A Pyramid of Deliverables

Begin with the Destination
A project plan represents how the team believes they can best get to the desired destination—a new product, an installed system, a new or renovated building, etc. It is fairly obvious that planning would begin by getting very clear about that destination. However, project teams in complex work environments rarely have the luxury to step back and look at the big picture. Planning for the *next* big project is often begun by people who are still primarily focused on the *last* big project. Because it is common for the next project to be similar in many ways to the previous one, the interesting aspects of planning will be those aspects of the next project that are different (e.g. new features, new tools and technologies) from the last. Although these conditions are distracting, they cannot become excuses for failing to begin the planning process with the end of the current project in mind. Hence, clarifying the destination must be deliberate, and begins by understanding who the customer is and what the project team is going to deliver to them (ultimate deliverable).

Ask five members of the project team who the key customer is and you are likely to get at least three different answers. *Customer* can be interpreted as paying customer, internal sponsor, internal downstream customer, a variety of different stakeholders and even stockholders. For the purpose of project planning, however, the team should focus on who will be taking delivery of the team's ultimate deliverable. But, it is common for the discussion to bounce back and forth between ultimate deliverable and key customers before both become crystal clear. Figure 15 shows some examples of team types, their ultimate deliverable and the likely customers on whom they need to focus.

The concrete pourers in the first example could view their customers as the home buyers, or the framers, plumbers and electricians that will build up from their foundations. However, the general contractor is paying the bill, and the site supervisor's job is to make sure the foundations meet the needs of the other subcontractors. In the office building example, there may be a variety of potential future occupants. But if 80 percent, or even 40 percent, of the building is going to be occupied by one tenant, it is probably valuable to identify that tenant as *the* customer in representation of all the smaller tenants. Likewise, for a new telephone switching system, a new release (SVR) may be sold to several carriers, but the one or two large carriers that have already committed to the new release (the targeted carriers) are the ones whose needs must be met, and they are worth calling out in the project plan. Those carriers' sustaining managers are also distinct customers, because if they determine the new system is too unreliable, or too hard to sustain, they can prevent acceptance of the system (and the sale).

Customer Deliverables

Defining the customer and ultimate deliverable are interim steps to agreeing on a complete list of "customer deliverables." The clearest statement of the destination of a project is a short list of "customer deliverables" and a few overall success measures for the project. Customer deliverables are the three to seven deliverables that the project team has contracted to provide to the key customers. This "contract" is sometimes formal and sometimes informal. If it is discovered that no such agreement with key customers exists at this stage in planning, one should be put in place. This is important because simply planning to produce the *ultimate* deliverable is almost always insufficient. For example, when you buy a new house, in addition to the house it is typical to expect warranties with any appliances, an agreement to fix anything that's not just right during the next several months, the lot to be graded (ready for landscaping), and a package of interior finishes. These, along with the house itself, are all examples of customer deliverables.

Team Type	Ultimate Deliverable	Key Customer(s)
Subcontracting concrete pourers	57 poured foundations for a new housing development	Site Supervisor for the general contracting firm
General contracting construction team	New office building	Property developer/manager representative for the primary occupants
Telephone switching system development team	System version release (SVR)—hardware and software that upgrades a switching system and enables new telephone features (e.g. voicemail, auto message send, etc.)	Network manager (person responsible for implementing new switching systems) for 1 or 2 targeted local exchange carrier(s) Sustaining manager (person responsible for maintaining the system)

Figure 15. Example Ultimate Deliverables and Customers

In the telephone switching system example (Figure 16), a local exchange carrier (telephone company) cannot and will not convert to a new system version release (SVR) unless it comes supported by early documentation about retrofitting existing equipment (Information Memorandum); the database conversion, which is used to tailor the SVR to system needs; and documents and online support to install and use the SVR. If a SVR development team fails to deliver any one of these items in a timely manner, they will not succeed overall.

If it is proving difficult to limit the list of customer deliverables to seven items or less, you are probably thinking at too detailed a level. The customer deliverables are just those things that will be delivered to the key customer. They tend to be things that emerge towards the end of the project, although there are often one or two exceptions to this. In the switching system example, the *information memorandum* enables the telephone company to prepare its peripheral systems for the incoming switching software. It is an

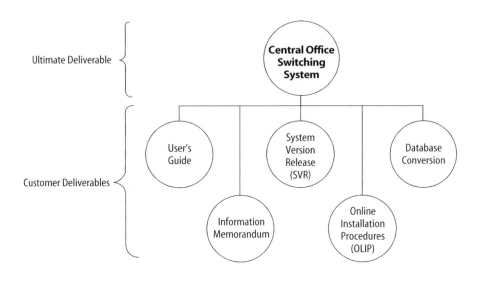

Figure 16. Example of Customer Deliverables for Telephone Switching System Project

example of a customer deliverable that must be delivered long before the project is over.

Project Measures of Success

The project's high-level measures of success should be clarified to complete the picture of the desired destination. High level means these are measures for the overall project. They are usually oriented towards aspects of the customer contract and the larger organization's business goals. High-level measures of success for the concrete pouring project might include $700 maximum cost per foundation and no more than one repour for all 57 lots. The published high-level measures of success for the Chunnel Project were that the tunnel would last 120 years, be resistant to terrorism, be exceptionally safe for humans and fatal for rabid animals. Example measures of success for the switching system example are as follows:

- Three new specified features (e.g., call waiting) are fully implemented

- System implemented without any "lines down" time

- 11 percent profit margin

Avoiding the Activity Trap

With the destination (customer deliverables and measures of success) clearly stated, planning can now be focused on how to get to the destination. For many experienced project participants, planning how to get from here to there conjures up visions of task-beginning and end dates, identifying concurrent tasks and detailed schedules based on task durations. Subteams and individuals may eventually choose to plan their own time in this manner. However, the project plan doesn't need to and shouldn't get bogged down in these details. Planning and tracking all the activities and time that each team member invests in the project does not provide the performance data (what's completed versus what was committed) that enables timely and sound decisions throughout the project. **The goal of project control is to make sure what the team has agreed to accomplish gets accomplished, not to make sure that subteams and individuals are following a specific predetermined task list.** The tribulations associated with trying to manage each individual down to the task level have been well documented by Odiorne[1] and Gilbert[2].

The alternative to specifying what everyone needs to *do* to get from here to there is to focus on what needs to be *produced*[3]. This is done most clearly in terms of "internal deliverables." Internal deliverables are never received (and often never even seen) by the customer, but they must be produced in order for the customer deliverables to be produced. In the concrete pourer example, the internal deliverables required to produce one poured foundation include: an accurate map of the property with lot numbers, available drivers, available concrete ingredients, available finishers and a poured foundation. If each of these internal deliverables is completed in a quality fashion (done and done well), a finished foundation (the customer deliverable) will result.

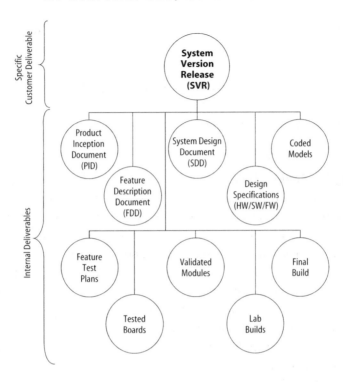

Figure 17. Example of Internal Deliverables for the SVR Customer Deliverable

In the switching system example, before a system version release can be delivered, there must be a system design document (SDD) based on a defined list of product features. The SDD supports the design specifications for hardware, software and firmware, which are required to produce a coded model of the SVR, test plans, etc. These are just some of the larger internal deliverables required to produce an SVR. It is equally important to identify internal deliverables for each of the remaining customer deliverables. The goal of this activity is to identify the necessary and sufficient internal deliverables at a high level. A good rule to follow is to limit internal deliverables to 8 to 12 for each customer deliverable at this stage. More detail can be added later if necessary.

The customer deliverables and high-level internal deliverables form what we call the *Pyramid of Deliverables* for the project. It is occasionally useful on very complex projects to expand the pyramid down one more level of detail (subinternal deliverables for each internal deliverable). However, it is recommended that you err on the side of less detail, and come back to add it later if necessary.

The Deliverables Map: Tipping Over the Pyramid

For some project teams, carrying out the planning described to this point may be rather uncomfortable the first time or two. Many people are unaccustomed to focusing on deliverables versus tasks and working vertically, down from the destination. But keep in mind that our goal of escaping the vicious cycle requires a commitment-based plan, and each of the steps, and the sequence described in this chapter, are critical to its development. However, commitment-based planning will be more comfortable for everyone when the pyramid of deliverables is "tipped over" to form a horizontal deliverables map. Figure 18 is an example of the front end of a deliverables map for a switching system project.

One of the best ways to tip over the pyramid of deliverables is to transcribe each deliverable onto a yellow sticky note and then place the deliverables on a long wall where they can be easily resequenced. As shown in the example, it is useful to divide the wall into rows representing different functional subteams who will produce those deliverables and columns based on a few major project milestones. Although the deliverables map does not have any dates on it yet, it is important when placing the deliverables to attempt to place them at the point they are going be completed (relative to other deliverables and the milestone reference points). The map now shows roughly where each major deliverable needs to be completed relative to all the other deliverables. The customer deliverables should also be included. Typically all but one or two will fall at the far right-hand side of the map (not shown in diagram).

The deliverables map is where we begin to define clear subteam and individual expectations for the project. But before beginning that process, the map should be reviewed carefully for any necessary internal deliverables that are missing. At this time, it is common to add more deliverables (usually 10 to 15 percent more). For example, some of the deliverables identified may in reality represent a series of drafts or revisions of a deliverable. In Figure 18, the system design diagram (SDD) is shown as a single deliverable, but in reality there are usually two to three revisions of the SDD. Each revision adds more detail to the design and enables another phase of devel-

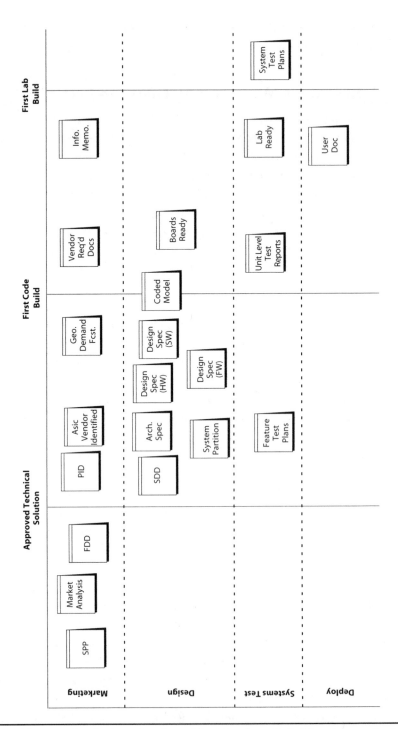

Figure 18. Example of a Partial Deliverables Map for a Switching-System Project

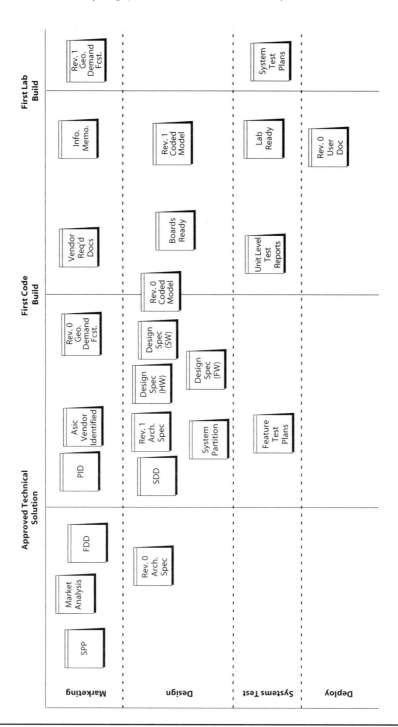

Figure 19. Deliverables Map with Revisions Added

opment. The deliverables map is where specific revisions and their location to other deliverables get specified (see Figure 19. Deliverables Map with Revisions Added). However, this is still not the place to conduct task-level planning. Most of the deliverables on the map should be ones that get passed on to one or more other functional subteams, as opposed to representing a series of steps performed *within* one functional subteam.

A Network of Customer-Supplier Relationships

When the deliverables map seems reasonably accurate and complete at a high level, it is time to identify project dependencies. The recommended approach is to identify one "owner" and one or more "users" for each deliverable on the map. Although many team members may contribute to any one deliverable, one person needs to take responsibility for owning each deliverable. The owner will be the person who reports progress for that specific deliverable. For this reason, subteam leaders are often owners for the majority of the deliverables on the map. However, if an individual contributor is the primary contributor and the most knowledgeable person in regards to a deliverable, he or she should, by all means, be the owner.

"Users" of a deliverable are team leaders and subteam members who are dependent upon that deliverable in order to make their contributions to the project. In the concrete pourer example, the site supervisor owns the task of providing the concrete contractor with an accurate map of the site. The truck drivers are some of the users of that map. If they don't get the map, or can't use the map, they may be delayed in finding the lots that need pouring on a specific day. In a sense, each owner-user relationship is a miniature customer-supplier relationship on the project. In regards to the site map, the site supervisor is a *supplier* to the truck drivers, who are his *customers*. This will be a useful way to think about dependencies for the next step in the process.

Dependencies can also be identified by drawing lines to connect appropriate deliverables on the map. However, it will still be necessary to specify owners and users on the deliverables matrix, so lines on the map do not provide sufficient detail.

At this stage, the deliverables map represents who needs to deliver what to whom and in what sequence, in order for all the customer deliverables to be produced. However, there are two more important components remaining:

"quality requirements" and "first-horizon commit dates." Because we are interested in a commitment-based plan, there is more value in focusing on the front end of the plan than trying to nail down the whole thing at this point. The front end of the deliverables map should be carefully reviewed to identify any holes or disconnects. (A hole might be a missing deliverable or one without a defined owner or users.) Now is the time to clarify who owns what deliverables. If a deliverable has been defined with an owner, but there are no users for the deliverable, maybe that deliverable should be removed from the map. This is called "validating the deliverables map," and it leaves just one critical step before attempting to apply any dates to the plan.

Quality Requirements: How Good is Good Enough?

For new product development, a product market forecast is a study done by marketing to estimate how many units of a new product will be sold and how much revenue they will likely generate. When asked to estimate the time required to develop a *good* product market forecast, a product marketing engineer replied, "At least two full weeks." When the same engineer was asked how he would know if a product market forecast was a good one, he stopped to think and then said, "A good product market forecast is one that is approved by the division manager." Through further inquiry, it was revealed that the division manager always had specific forecast numbers in mind (ones consistent with her financial objectives) and that the provided forecast, no matter how rigorously developed, was always simply "judged" up or down to meet the division manager's financial plan.

This true anecdote demonstrates how getting clear about the required quality of specific project deliverables can reduce the amount of work required. Given the scenario, any time spent by product marketing engineers perfecting their estimated forecasts was a waste of time. Time would be better spent finding out what the division manager wanted to see in the forecast and quickly matching the analysis to that forecast. This may not be the best way to do forecasting, but it was the smartest way in this particular environment. It is quite common for performers to build quality and elegance into internal deliverables that aren't valued by the "users" of that deliverable. This phenomenon is sometimes called "creeping elegance" and is often a factor in preventing project teams from achieving their ultimate goals. However, creeping elegance can be reduced by predefining quality requirements for each internal deliverable.

As Ted's team learned, clarifying internal deliverable quality criteria is also the most effective way to combat cross-functional finger pointing—when functional subteams accuse each other of sending on shoddy work. When there is no up-front discussion about the quality of specific internal deliverables, it is all too easy for a "downstream" subteam to blame their slow progress on the subpar deliverables they received from other subteams.

Having subteams communicate clearly with each other about quality expectations is very difficult when plans are task based. For example, to talk about quality concrete pouring we need to begin to analyze how different pourers do their jobs. However, if we focus the conversation on deliverables, we can clarify the criteria for a poured foundation without any arguments about the "one best way" to pour a foundation. Good poured foundations are level to one quarter inch per ten-foot diameter and have no cracks more than an eighth inch thick. If the pourers, the finishers and the site supervisor agree on these criteria at the outset, the chances of disputes are much smaller. More importantly, the owners of this deliverable are focused on the right things each time they pour and finish a foundation, so they are more likely to do it right the first time, and to not waste time striving for perfection (perfectly level with no cracks at all).

Defining "good enough" involves making sure that the owner and users of each internal deliverable discuss and agree to specific quality requirements *before* work begins on that deliverable. Figure 20 is an example of quality requirements for the internal deliverable, the product name for the new SVR, from the telephone switching system example. In the example, system administrators need an internal name for new products that meet certain tracking system requirements. Marketing, the other primary user of the SVR name, is concerned about positioning the new SVR in relation to other related products and catching the attention of targeted customers.

Don't get bogged down trying to define a perfect set of measures of quality; they are only intended to clarify the requirements. If they are really measured and tracked, it will probably be by the owners for their own self-monitoring purposes. The most useful measures are "leading" rather than "lagging." Leading measures are those that are apparent while the person is doing the work. "Product names must load into the system" is an example. If the person naming the product knows the system requirements, it is within his or her control to come up with a name that meets those criteria. Lagging measures

Internal Deliverable: Product Name for New SVR

Content:

    External name

    Internal name

Quality:	**Measures:**
External meets marketing Reqs	*Approved by VP of Mrktg*
Internal follows tracking convention	*Loads into tracking system*
Internal uses accurate descriptors	*Descriptors follow naming spec*

Figure 20. Quality Requirements for the Internal Deliverable

are those that won't be apparent until the project, or a major phase of the project, is complete. A nonproject-oriented example of lagging measures would be the watering eyes, the difficulty in breathing, and the sharp burning sensation experienced when you eat really hot peppers. But once you've experienced that, it's a little too late. Wouldn't it be better to know that those red and black wrinkly things are killer peppers before you dig in to that kung pao shrimp? Measures must inform owners, *ahead of time*, of what they need to do to satisfy their users and ensure their own success.

Making a list containing content requirements, quality requirements and measures is just one suggested way to have owners and users structure their conversation about quality requirements. An even simpler alternative is to have owners and users brainstorm what a specific deliverable "is" and "is not", and then agree upon the statements that best describe the desired outcome. The important thing is that owners and users have these conversations before work on the deliverable gets very far along.

This part of project planning recognizes that each dependency in a project plan is a customer-supplier relationship. The quality movement teaches that a key component of pleasing your customers is listening to them. Essentially, this component of planning ensures that all the owners of specific internal deliverables know who their users are, and that they listen to them before it's too late to do things right the first time.

First-Horizon Commits: The Goal of the Planning Process

When it is clear who needs to deliver what to whom, and how good each internal deliverable needs to be, it is finally time to start discussing dates. The discussion can include estimating, but it needs to eventually result in owner and subteam commitments. Remember, after the deliverables map was validated, attention turned to the front portion of the map. This is because team members are unlikely to have all the information (or confidence in themselves) they need to make commitments further out on the timeline where uncertainty clouds the picture. The portion of the deliverables map that is understood with clarity is sometimes called the project horizon. In the initial stages of project planning, the goal is to get solid commitments for completing the deliverables in the first project horizon, or "first-horizon commits."

The first horizon for Ted's team was through completion of the architecture document, which turned out to be about five weeks. The team members argued that uncertainty was much greater beyond the document because it was during development of the architecture that the team would "discover" the best approach for designing the chipset. Ted was anxious to get dates committed for several project milestones, but he wisely let the team decide how far out they could make commitments. **It is much more important to have a real commitment to a few deliverable dates than to find out later that team members felt pressured to promise dates they knew couldn't be achieved.**

The question that needs to be posed to deliverable owners and their subteams is: "When can you commit to finish your deliverable to the specified quality criteria?" As subteams are coming up with their answers to this question, they should document any important assumptions built into their commitments. For example: Is the team assuming they will produce the deliverable with current resources, or that they will get additional ones? and What are the key tactics the team plans to use to accomplish this deliverable? These assumptions about how the deliverable can best be produced may be asked for later in the process if the subteam's commitments are poorly aligned with the milestone date, based on the top-down request date.

This is the one time in the commitment-based planning process when subteams and individuals are encouraged to plan their own work down to the task level. However, these details will still not be documented in the project plan. Their purpose is to coordinate work within the subteam and to ensure that each individual knows if he or she is on track to complete deliverables when committed. Therefore, these detailed plans should be owned and managed by the subteam members.

First-horizon commit dates can be applied directly to the deliverables map in order to get a sense of the high-level schedule that is evolving from the planning process. This is also an appropriate time to see how the bottom-up schedule is aligning to the top-down request date. It is usually not too difficult for the leadership team to work backwards from the top-down request date and apply dates to key project milestones. This is, after all, the way vicious cycle teams usually *begin* planning. Figures 21 and 22 are examples of what the deliverables map might look like at this final stage of initial commitment-based planning.

As in these hypothetical examples, it can often be determined at this stage whether the bottom-up commits are reasonably aligned to the top-down request date. The foundation-pouring plan looks reasonably aligned, but the telephone switching system project has at least one issue. If the Rev. 1 architecture spec isn't completed until workweek 15, there will not be adequate time to complete the Design Specs and Rev. 0 coded model of the chip by workweek 18. When one or more dates are clearly out of line, it is prudent to reconcile the major differences immediately. To a large extent, how this is handled determines if the project team will or will not be committed to the project plan. But before describing the recommendations for handling this process, it is important to understand how to involve the entire project team in coming up with deliverable commitments.

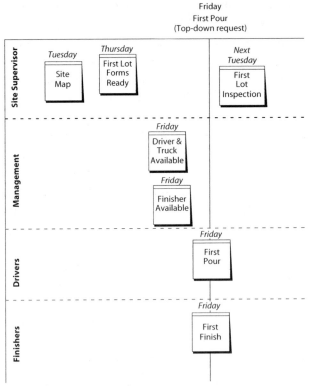

Note: Commit dates listed above each deliverable (e.g. Tuesday)

Figure 21. Example of Deliverables Map with First-Horizon Commits and Top-Down Request Dates

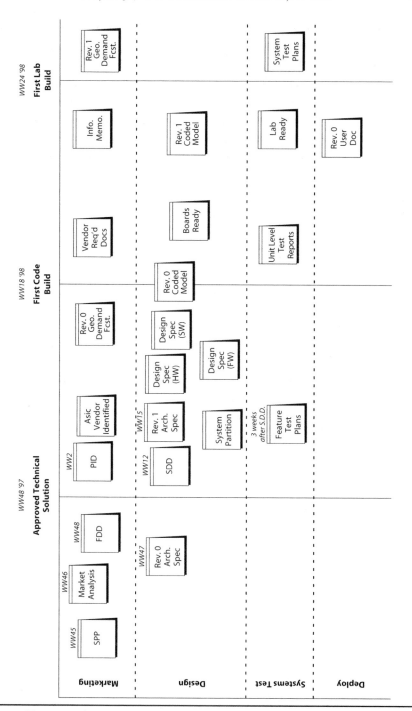

Figure 22. Example of a Complex Project with Bottom-up Commits (for Specific Deliverables) and Top-down Request Dates (for Major Milestones)

Whereas task-based planning is focused on coming up with a detailed schedule and a forecasted end date for a project, commitment-based planning is focused on providing a simple and accurate high-level plan and, at the same time, building whole team commitment to that plan. This chapter has identified the key ingredients to commitment-based plans. Some of the differences between conventional project planning and commitment-based planning are rather subtle. However, if you and your team are often surprised by schedule slips that become apparent just as milestones are supposed to be completed, it would behoove you to note the differences and focus on them.

This chapter has focused on the first two simple rules for commitment-based planning:

1. Plans are stated in terms of who is delivering what to whom, and when (deliverables versus tasks).

2. Quality requirements are predefined for each deliverable before dates are committed.

The next chapter will describe how to accomplish commitment-based planning very rapidly while following Planning Rule #3: *Whoever will execute the plan needs to participate in developing the plan.*

Summary

- Each individual needs to participate in setting his or her own performance goals. Project managers and team leaders cannot make commitments for others.

- The outcome of commitment-based planning is a high-level plan with dates for specific deliverables for the first project horizon.

- The team's high-level plan is represented in the form of a deliverables matrix.

- Commitment-based planning includes the following components in sequence:

  — The ultimate deliverable

  — Customers

  — High-level measure of success

  — Customer deliverables

  — Internal deliverables

  — The deliverables map

  — Internal-deliverable quality criteria

  — First-horizon commits.

- Commitment-based planning can and should be done very rapidly and with full team participation.

1. George S. Odiorne, *Management and the Activity Trap* (New York: Harper and Row, 1972).

2. Thomas F. Gilbert, *Human Competence: Engineering Worthy Performance*, Tribute Edition (Washington DC: The International Society of Performance Improvement, 1996).

3. Andrew S. Grove, *High Output Management* (New York: Random House, 1983).

Team Planning Meetings

T his chapter will describe the "team planning meeting"—the first of three types of meetings that get the right people talking about the right things at the right time. It is where all contributors to the project begin getting committed to a single project plan. Getting team members truly committed to a project plan is the first necessary step towards helping the organization emerge from the project management vicious cycle. The question is, how can a meeting possibly be productive with 30, 60 or 100 participants?

In 1991, the Sematech consortium (formed to ensure that the US did not lose technical superiority in semiconductor technology) arranged a series of seminars on project management techniques. The main presenter was one of the leaders of the successful Polaris missile submarine program referenced in Chapter 1.* Rick Dehmel, an Intel representative at Sematech at the time, attended the seminars hoping to find some tools and techniques that would transfer to the complex world of integrated electronics development.

*The "Polaris" presenter is retired and asked not to be named.

The most significant technique that emerged from the seminars came to be known at Intel as Map Day.[1] Map Day is a meeting process for involving the entire project team in project planning. There are some significant differences between developing new systems in the military and developing new products in the private sector, but there are also similarities. Dehmel says that Map Day "emerged from the lessons learned on the Polaris program, after stripping away everything that had to do with government bureaucracy and compartmentalization, and adding some of the latest techniques for effective group process". The team planning meeting described in this chapter is an adaptation of the Map Day concept designed to ensure that the project plan is a commitment-based plan.

The previous chapter identified the necessary components and the sequence for commitment-based planning. This chapter focuses on doing it rapidly and with full team participation. To accomplish this, team leaders need to understand some things about assumptions.

Towards Shared Assumptions

Whenever a group of people is assembled to accomplish something together, each individual begins with his own assumptions about how to go about implementation. Some people's assumptions will be focused on local and tactical issues. For example, one cement truck driver's assumptions about pouring foundations might focus on the appropriate mix of ingredients or the appropriate speed of pouring. Another driver might have more strategic assumptions, such as the number of foundations that can be poured in a day or how to best schedule all the pouring jobs in a given week or month. In this same example, the truck driver's manager probably has some broad assumptions regarding the best overall strategy for achieving the goal of 57 foundations poured on schedule with no more than one repour. The one thing you can count on is that everyone will have some assumptions. And there's also a good chance that many of these assumptions won't be completely aligned with each other.

Building team commitment to a plan is about making sure that people's assumptions get shared and tested, and that the team moves toward one set of shared assumptions. Testing assumptions involves asking questions about someone else's assertions to make sure you understand them, and then if you disagree, explaining why. The goal is to get whatever data people have regarding these assumptions out in the open so it can be considered before a decision is made to follow one set of assumptions or another. **It is not necessary to achieve consensus on all decisions in order for the team to get committed to the plan.** But it is necessary that members of the team feel they've had the opportunity to share their personal assumptions and test those most different from their own. In addition to building commitment, sharing and testing assumptions produces a tremendous amount of learning, usually in the form of issues that will need attention in order for the team to be successful. The objectives of the team planning meeting are to:

- move toward a set of mostly shared assumptions,

- understand and document issues that arise as assumptions are shared and tested,

- clarify cross-functional expectations and

- build whole team commitment to the resulting project plan.

Appendix 1 provides a detailed guide for facilitating the team planning meeting. This chapter describes several considerations for making sure your team planning meetings yield commitment-based plans.

When and How to Begin Planning

Complex projects are typically managed in phases. Proposal, definition, design, validation, build and sustaining are commonly used terms for these phases on new product development projects. The phase names may be different in competitive bidding environments (e.g. definition is analogous to design and implementation is analogous to construction), but the idea is the same. Although team planning meetings that are focused on getting to a project definition have proven quite valuable, team planning is most crucial when planning the last four phases—development through sustaining. These are often the phases where the largest number of people will be contributing to the project. For purposes of illustration, we will assume that this is where whole team planning is going to begin.

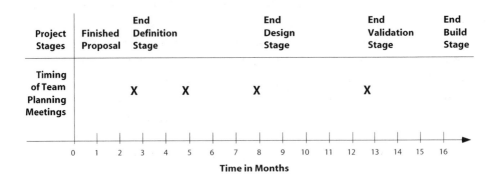

Figure 23. Typical Timing of Team Planning Meetings on a Complex Project

In Figure 23, note that the project horizon (represented here by the length of time between team planning meetings) gets longer as the project progresses. This is partly due to the fact that uncertainty is decreasing, and teams can see further down the path with clarity. But another important factor is that teams build confidence as they meet their own commitments. The more confidence the team has in itself, the further out it will be willing to make personal commitments. It is the commitment-based approach that will best improve confidence and trust over time, so in the early stages, management needs to rely on the team members to determine how far out they can make commitments.

Another general rule for when to hold the first team-planning meeting is when the project is about 25 percent staffed. Although it has been implied that all contributors to a project should participate in every team planning meeting, that is not exactly what usually occurs. What's most important is that *every project function is represented* in each team planning meeting (preferably by both leaders and one or two individual contributors), and that *every contributor from the current phase of the project attends.* This means that the first team-planning meeting will likely need to be attended by all members of those subteams heavily involved in the design phase. But only representatives will be needed from the teams more involved with validation, build and sustaining. Likewise, later meetings may have a few representatives from subteams most focused on design, and full participation from subteams focused on validation and build. The result is that all team members participate in the planning process over the course of the project, but the whole team is never in attendance at any one meeting. Therefore, even teams with 100 to 200 contributors will have closer to 60 to 80 people at any one team planning meeting, which is quite manageable if the meeting is planned and structured properly.

Preparation for the Team Planning Meeting

The majority of meeting participants will not need to do any preparation for the initial team-planning meeting. In fact, if this is the first time using a commitment-based approach, it is better that not too much planning be done prior to the meeting. This is because team members are usually most familiar with task-based planning, but the goal of team planning meetings is to get team members focused on deliverables first. However, the *owners* of the meeting do need to prepare, especially when they are just starting to use the commitment-based approach.

Typically, the meeting is ultimately owned by the overall project manager, although he or she may delegate preparations for the meeting to someone else. When using this approach for the first time, it is important that all members of the project leadership team be informed and committed to it; therefore, a preplanning meeting for team leaders is recommended. This is where the project leadership reaches a set of shared assumptions regarding the project's ultimate deliverable, the customer and the high-level measures of success discussed in Chapter 3. A team preplanning meeting template (provided in the appendix as a template with a completed example) guides you through:

- clarifying the customer, customer deliverable and high-level success criteria (to be used in the sponsor presentation);

- agreeing on the meeting objectives;

Day 1

Item	Activity	Outcome	Est. Time
1	Sponsor Presentation	Define customer, ultimate project deliverable and high level measures of success.	10 min.
2	Housekeeping: Warm-Up Activity Meeting Agenda/Roles Ground Rules	Clear expectations for this meeting.	50 min.
3	Define Customer Deliverables (Plus Break)	3-7 tangible things we will deliver to the customer(s).	70 min.
4	Define Internal Deliverables (Plus Break)	8-12 major things that must be produced along the way to deliver each customer deliverable.	100 min.
5	Validate the Deliverables Map (parallel activity: Past Lessons Learned)	Sequence of events: who will deliver what to whom. (What lessons from the past can help us perform better on this project?)	60 min.

Figure 24a. Example of a Two-Day Agenda for a Team Planning Meeting

- agreeing on the meeting agenda;

- agreeing on key meeting roles and

- making sure meeting logistics are covered.

One way to reduce the preparation time for the project manager and project leaders is to have a professional facilitator take responsibility for planning and facilitating the team planning meeting. The facilitator's role is to lead

Day 2

Item	Activity	Outcome	Est. Time
6	Walk through the Map (Plus Break)	Identify holes and disconnects. Identify the rough critical path.	70 min.
7	Define Internal Deliverables Quality Requirements (Plus Break)	How we'll know if each internal deliverable is done and done well.	130 min.
8	Make First-Horizon Commitments	When teams can commit to deliver specific early deliverables.	60 min.
9	Wrap-up/Next Steps	Issues turned into actions, and expectations about what the team will do with meeting outcomes.	30 min.
10	Reconcile First Commits to Top-Down Schedule	The deliverables matrix	varies

Figure 24b. Example of a Two-Day Agenda for a Team Planning Meeting

the participants through the meeting exercises, make sure the group's ground rules are kept in front of them and keep the meeting focused on the stated objectives. Thus, it is very difficult for one person to do a good job as both the meeting driver and the meeting facilitator because the roles have very different purposes. If a professional facilitator is not available, someone other than the meeting driver and, preferably, someone that has no role on this project, should take responsibility for facilitation. Some organizations have managers of different projects facilitate each other's team planning meetings.

Whoever the facilitator is, he or she will need adequate preparation time to learn the approach and to collect appropriate materials, so this decision should be made at least a few weeks before a team planning meeting.

A week or so before the team planning meeting, it is a good idea to send at least a rough draft of the meeting agenda to all participants so they will realize that the meeting is not about each subteam presenting and defending their plans. Figures 24a and 24b show a detailed agenda for a two-day team planning meeting. In the "Activity" column you will recognize most of the components of commitment-based planning outlined in the previous chapter (components not in Activity column are treated as givens and presented in the sponsor presentation).

Setting the Meeting Up for Success

Although the core of commitment-based planning occurs in items 3 to 8, the first two items are extremely important for ensuring a successful meeting. Having a high-level sponsor present to kick off the meeting adds legitimacy to the project and, when done well, clarifies for all project participants how this project fits into the strategic objectives of the organization. The project destination (in terms of ultimate deliverable, customers and high-level measures of success) should also be briefly presented by the sponsor. A brief and crisp sponsor presentation ensures that team members are listening passively for only a few minutes before getting into a participative part of the meeting. It puts a real damper on your participative meeting when the first 30 to 45 minutes are spent listening to a poorly prepared sponsor "ramble on" or field endless questions that are going to be addressed in the body of the meeting.

Even after a good crisp sponsor presentation, it is important to get all participants involved as soon as possible. The warm-up activity in the "housekeeping" portion of the meeting will do just that. The important thing about a warm-up activity is that everyone gets to participate on an equal footing. The goal is for all meeting participants to have an equal voice in the meeting. Everyone's opinions are worth listening to and the assumptions behind those opinions need to be tested. If you want participation from everyone later, they need to feel included immediately (hence, these activities are sometimes called *inclusion activities*).[2] Although there are almost unlimited ways to get the group warmed up, the following warm-up activity is designed not only to include everybody, but also to present some concepts that are important throughout a team planning meeting. It is strongly recommended that teams new to this process begin with this activity.

Example Warm-Up Activity: Foundation-Pouring Project

In small groups, determine if each numbered item is a "deliverable" or a "task."

1. Drive truck from the quarry to the housing development

2. Map showing lot locations

3. Ingredients mixed and ready to pour

4. Poured foundation

5. Dig the trenches for the forms

6. Review and approve the weekly pouring schedule

7. All 57 lots poured

8. Send invoices to the site supervisor

9. Smooth out the wet concrete

10. Inspect foundation after it dries

Notice that items two, three, four and seven are more output-oriented compared to the rest. They describe deliverables rather than the activities or tasks required to produce deliverables. This is the distinction you want the team members to discover and discuss during the warm-up activity. It is also recommended that someone prepare a list of items relevant to the specific project being planned. So, for example, the items used with the team planning to develop a new telephone switching system would look more like the following. (You will eventually need to come up with alternative warm-up activities for teams experienced with this approach.)

Example Items for Warm-Up Activity: Telephone Switching System Project

1. Spec writing

2. Market analysis

3. Write code

4. System partition

5. Feature test plans

6. Install tools in the lab

7. Vendors identified

8. Publish unit level test results

9. Coded model

10. First lab build

After the warm-up activity, participants need to understand the objectives of the meeting and the general agenda for the day. Then there is one more critical housekeeping activity before the body of the meeting.

Towards Shared Assumptions in a Large Group

Meeting Ground Rules

It is easy to talk about moving towards shared assumptions, but it doesn't happen automatically by getting a bunch of people in a room. Each portion of the meeting can be structured to encourage participants to share assumptions, but in order to get people actively testing assumptions, you may have to give them permission. This can be done during the "housekeeping" portion of the meeting by spending a few minutes agreeing on ground rules for behavior in the meeting. Three recommended ground rules are:

- when you hear an assumption you don't share, test it;

- before you test an assumption, seek to understand it; and

- test ideas and assumptions but not the individuals who say them.

Because teams operating in the vicious cycle have often developed bad habits in regards to respecting each other's assumptions, these three ground rules are designed to make sure assumptions are tested and that it is always done with respect for the other person. Treating each other with respect is important, because when members of the group fail to do it many people will stop sharing and testing assumptions. **You can count on assumptions that go unspoken and untested to show up as unwelcome surprises later in the project.**

Encouraging the Sharing of Assumptions—the Dump and Clump

The ground rules set the team up to test each other's assumptions regarding the next four items on the agenda: customer deliverables, internal deliverables, the deliverables map and internal-deliverable quality requirements. For three of these four items, a specific group process is recommended to encourage the participants to share their assumptions in the first place. This process is called the "Dump and Clump."* In each case, the participants are organized into small groups. (This is only a conceptual overview; details for facilitating each item on the agenda are provided in the appendix.) Each member of each small group is provided with a stack of yellow sticky notes and told to brainstorm and write down one idea per sticky note until they are done. For example, during item 3 on the agenda—customer deliverables—each member of each small group is simultaneously brainstorming what the customer deliverables are for the whole project and writing each deliverable on a sticky note. The members of each small group then gather around a flat surface (a nearby wall, flipchart, etc.) and "dump" all their sticky notes onto it (see Figure 25 for an example of dumping). Working together, with lots of questions that clarify and test assumptions, each team "clumps" the

---

* A term that apparently emerged when Rick Dehmel and Bill Daniels were creating the Map Day concept.

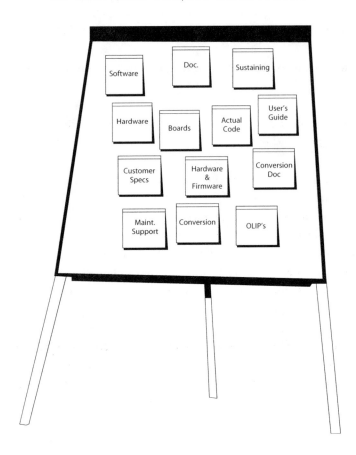

Figure 25. Example Output of Dumping Customer Deliverables for Telephone Switching System

similar ideas together. (See Figure 26 for an example of clumping.) Finally, when all agree that the clumps are mutually exclusive, and each clump is a legitimate customer deliverable, each clump is given a label. Each small group now has a set of shared assumptions regarding the customer deliverables for the project.

In the example, the small group ended up with four clumps and some ambiguity about what to do with documentation. Also, this particular group separated out hardware and software into two separate customer deliverables rather than combining them into the SVR deliverable. To move from small-group shared assumptions to whole-group shared assumptions, each group would report on their labels and eliminate the duplicates. Then,

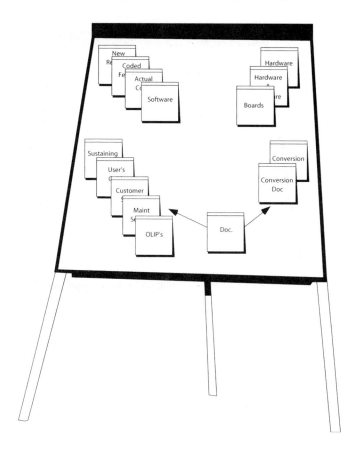

Figure 26. Example Output of Clumping Customer Deliverables for Telephone Switching System

working as a whole project team, the large group tests the assumptions that went into the combined list of customer deliverables and refines that list until it meets the criteria for customer deliverables provided in Chapter 3 (see Figure 27). The remaining list is a set of shared assumptions about the customer deliverables for this project. Another dump and clump exercise can now be used to define the internal deliverables, and so on.

Shared assumptions about the deliverables map (item 4 on the agenda) are achieved through an exercise sometimes called the "flea market," which is described in detail in the appendix. What's important to understand here is that it is just another way of moving from individual assumptions to shared assumptions.

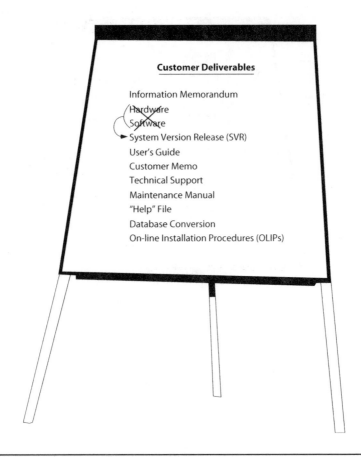

Figure 27. Refined List of Customer Deliverables

It is fairly common these days for people to assemble in groups and use sticky notes to diagram out a process or project, the solution to a specific problem or even organizational objectives. But many times the objective of those meetings is very different from what we are trying to achieve here. Unless all the right people are allowed to participate, the structure of the meeting encourages everyone to share and test assumptions *and* a distinction is made between commitments versus estimates, goals and plans, these meetings are not likely to achieve the stated objectives of the team planning meeting. As a result, your team is not likely to use the outcomes of these meetings to escape from the vicious cycle.

Towards Commitments Based on Shared Assumptions
Making Decisions
Throughout the meeting, as assumptions are being shared and tested, there will be many times when the large group does not reach consensus on which assumptions to adopt and, therefore, how to plan. When using a consensus approach to decision making, the team must agree that whenever *anyone* disagrees, the team will settle for the status quo.[3] At this stage in a project, the status quo is that there is no agreed upon plan—which is unacceptable!

An alternative form of decision making is the consultative process. When the consultative process is used, all meeting participants are viewed as consultants to one designated decision maker (also called the "meeting driver"), who is usually the project manager. This is a key role in the team planning meeting and the one exception to everyone participating on an equal footing. As issues arise, any participants that have relevant data and/or opinions share them. Anyone can test the assumptions inherent in the opinions offered, but the meeting driver ultimately weighs all the input and then makes a decision.

Note that the decisions made by the meeting driver are about how the team will coordinate their efforts to achieve the overall project goals. These decisions are different from the commitments that individuals and subteams need to make at the end of the meeting. Remember that people can only commit themselves, they cannot be committed by others.

Making Commitments
If the group process techniques described so far have been followed, by the time the group reaches item 8 on the agenda, the team has a set of shared assumptions. These assumptions delineate what needs to be delivered, to whom, and how good specific deliverables need to be in order to reach the project destination (delivery of the customer deliverables). The activity for item 8 is for subteams to assemble to determine when they can commit to provide the deliverables they own in the first project horizon.

Remember that the first project horizon (i.e., how far out on the map people can see clearly and plan effectively) is determined by the team members. Usually the horizon is defined relative to the most labor-intensive deliverables. Going back to Ted's case, most of the labor on the front end of the chipset development plan had to do with chipset design deliverables: the

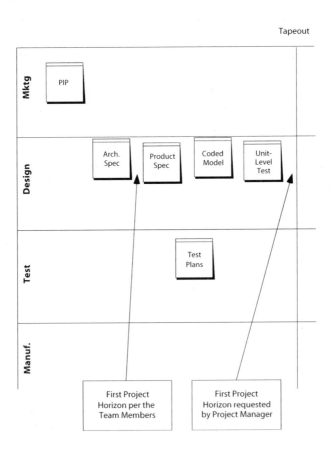

Figure 28. First Project Horizon

architecture document, specifications, the coded chip model and the tested chip model. In the first team-planning meeting, Ted asked each design subteam for commit dates on each deliverable up through chip-model coding, but they said they could see clearly only up through completion of the architecture document. However, in the second team-planning meeting, after the architecture document was complete, they were willing to set commit dates up through the first major milestone (tapeout).

While the subteams are working on their specific deliverable commit dates, the project manager can be applying dates to the major milestones on the deliverables map. These dates are estimates of when milestones need to be achieved in order to attain the top-down request date (or the contracted end date on a competitive bidding project). In this way, when the subteams post their commit dates on the map, everyone will be able to see if there is a serious mismatch between the early top-down milestone dates and the bottom-up subteam commitments. This analysis needs to focus on those deliverables that are relatively labor-intensive, or that constrain labor-intensive ones. This determination is similar to, but not the same as, a critical path analysis. Critical path requires knowledge of task start dates and durations, which the teams haven't necessarily defined in order to make commitments.

If one or more commit dates are driving the plan way out of alignment from the top-down request date, project management will need to work with those subteams to see if the detailed plans for those deliverables can be reconciled closer to the top-down driven milestone dates. This will probably require making some trade-offs. It is ideal if these trade-offs can be identified, and the first horizon commits can be finalized in the team planning meeting. But having these conversations in front of the entire team requires a high level of trust and team maturity, which is usually not present in teams that have been struggling in the vicious cycle. Therefore, it is common for this process to be handled in separate meetings with just the affected subteams, a day or two after the team planning meeting. This step of formalizing commitments, and beginning to make trade-offs (referred to as reconciliation) is a crucial point in the development of a commitment-based plan. A recommended approach to the reconciliation process will be described after some discussion about trade-offs.

A Few Words about Trade-offs

The project "performance triangle"[4] is still one of the most powerful concepts of project management. The performance triangle recognizes the inter-connected relationship between the scope of a project, how long it will last and the resources needed to complete it.

The lesson of the performance triangle is that whenever any one of the three variables (scope, time or resources) changes, you must recognize the impact on one or both of the other two variables. This is possibly the most basic and most ignored rule of effective project management. It is ignored every time a team member says, "That task took a little longer than expected, but I'll make it up on future tasks." It is ignored every time a team sets a schedule without first defining quality requirements for each internal deliverable. It is ignored every time a team falls behind its hiring-ramp plan but fails to adjust its schedule or scope accordingly. And these are just a few of the ways teams ignore one of the most basic rules of project management.

Every opportunity to follow or ignore this basic rule is called a trade-off (the term trade-off implies a certain type of decision). Trade-offs occur because plans are not perfect. At various points in a project it becomes apparent that the planned combination of scope, time and resources either cannot be achieved or will not result in meeting the project business goals. Plans are imperfect because of uncertainty. Complex projects are by defin-ition high in uncertainty. Therefore, complex projects have the most opportunities to follow or ignore the basic rule.

Trade-off opportunities occur frequently, and trade-offs are often made at each opportunity. However, team leadership usually recognizes only a few major trade-offs, usually rather deep into a project. For teams operating in the vicious cycle, this would be during crunch time (recall the case study from Chapter 1). When project members realized they were not going to meet task deadlines, one of the first tactics was to take shortcuts or to declare tasks done that clearly needed more work—the hope being that the task could be "shored up" later in the project. On the vicious cycle diagram (Figure 2), this practice is identified as "trading off quality (or scope) for schedule." This is an example of a trade-off that is not visible to, or recognized by, the leadership of the team. When teams are operating in a vicious-cycle envi-ronment, revealing trade-offs early in the project (or any other time) is

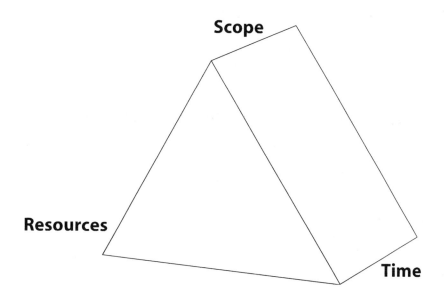

Figure 29. The Performance Triangle

Adapted, by permission, from Kerzner, *Project Management: A Systems Approach to Planning, Scheduling and Controlling, 2nd Edition.* Copyright © 1984 John Wiley & Sons, Inc.

strongly discouraged. The trade-offs still happen, but they are not revealed and comprehended by the system being used to manage the project.

Even when trade-offs become visible, there are sometimes pressures that make it difficult for leadership to make appropriate trade-off decisions. Unfortunately, ignoring early trade-offs makes it even harder to address them effectively later in the project. You've probably heard the expression about project managers making the "big bucks" because they make those "tough trade-off decisions." One reason the visible decisions are sometimes so tough is because of all the previous trade-offs that were ignored.

An important part of effective project management is making trade-offs visible. When this happens they are less likely to be ignored and more likely to be acted upon with valuable contributions from more people (for example downstream project members that will be affected if quality is traded off on a specific task deliverable). An effective performance system makes sure that early trade-offs are just as visible as those deeper into the project. (Chapter 5 will describe how to run progress review meetings that form the basis of a project-level performance system.) The first trade-offs that need to be visible are those that are made when the bottom-up commitments are being reconciled with a project's top-down request date.

Reconciling Bottom-up and Top-down Schedules

The longer it takes from the end of the team planning meeting to the point of having a performance system in place and operating, the greater the chance of succumbing to the early traps of the *vicious cycle*. It is recommended that project leadership work with subteams whose commit dates are out of alignment with the top-down request date within 48 hours of the team planning meeting (if it can't be done in the team planning meeting). The subteams will need to be prepared to share the assumptions they are using to define their commit dates. The reconciliation meeting should occur as soon as they are prepared.

The tone of the reconciliation meeting is critical. If subteam members believe that they are simply being pressured to pull in their commit dates without any trade-offs or changes in assumptions, commitment will be lost. Therefore, the following questions need to be answered in this meeting:

1 Are any of the basic assumptions used to make the commitment based on lack of, or incorrect, data or inconsistent with recent past history (in other words, the subteam's assumptions need to be tested)? If so, does correcting these assumptions better align the commit date to the top-down request date?

2 What can the team commit to after any adjustments to assumptions, scope or resources have been made?

3 What would it take for the team to be able to commit to a more aligned date? For example, should a product feature be eliminated, or should resources be added or acquired and brought up to speed faster?

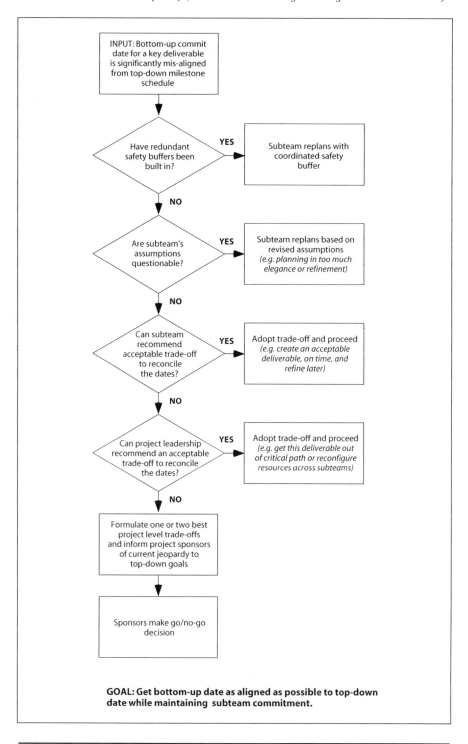

Figure 30. Reconciliation-Decision Diagram

Determining how much a first-horizon commit date must be pulled in to "align" with the top-down date is somewhat of an art. As previously discussed, the top-down request is only an educated guess. It may have a 10 to 20 percent *safety buffer* built into it as well (in this case *buffer* would mean a more aggressive date than needed). Extrapolating downstream milestone dates based on first-horizon commit dates also involves educated guesswork. Therefore, at the early stages of the project, leadership should only be concerned about significant misalignment. There should be an attempt to bring troublesome commits more into alignment, but not to the extent that subteams are no longer committed to their dates.

When subteams are asked to reexamine their assumptions, it is not uncommon for them to realize they have built inordinate "safety" into their commitment.[5] This can take several forms. Remember the case in Chapter 1: the subteam built safety into the plan by pulling tasks from a downstream deliverable (coded model) into an early deliverable (architecture specification). Occasionally, time estimates include redundant safety buffers (each team member adds some buffer to their part and then the subteam leader adds more buffer, for example). When this is the case, the role of the project manager is to help the subteam *choose* to remove unnecessary buffer. This must be a rational choice on the part of the team members. If they feel forced to eliminate what they believe is a prudent safety buffer, their commitment will be lost. Figure 30 provides a summary of the recommended questions and decisions that should be addressed when reconciling bottom-up commitments to a top-down request date.

Tough Trade-offs

If the answer to each of these questions is "no," and the overall projected date is significantly misaligned from the top-down request, now is the time to warn the project sponsors that the overall project goals are in jeopardy. Be prepared to provide the information that you asked your subteam to provide to you. You will need to demonstrate that you came to your conclusion only after due diligence. You should also be prepared to recommend the one or two trade-offs that would least affect the business goals of the project and still allow the project members to be committed to their dates. Appendix 1 provides the trade-off matrix for relating this conversation to the project triangle.

This is not a fun way to begin an exciting new project. But of course the alternative is to simply keep trade-offs invisible to the sponsors until they are so damaging to the business goals that they can no longer be hidden. Project managers often survive these nasty situations by blaming failure on the subteams that did not reveal their trade-offs throughout the project. But this is only fair if the project manager, all along, actively encouraged everyone to reveal them. The bottom line is that the effective project manager models making trade-offs visible. Chapter 7 advises project sponsors to respond appropriately when painful trade-offs are revealed to them. They have the same choice as do project managers: get reliable information throughout a project and have the opportunity to make trade-off decisions, or never know if a project is a business disaster until most of the resources have already been wasted.

Reconciling a subteam's early commitments with the top-down request date is one of the first opportunities on a project to set the tone of whether trade-offs are going to be concealed or revealed. Project teams will pick up on this tone very quickly and begin acting accordingly. Therefore, **the reconciliation process is a tremendous opportunity for the project leadership members to avoid, or begin to emerge from, the vicious cycle.**

Reconciliation is not over in those days following the first team-planning meeting. It is a process that will need to be repeated each time the team validates the plan for the next project horizon and makes deliverable commitments. However, the first reconciliation is often the most difficult, due to the fact that the team hasn't had a chance to build confidence about their ability to meet their own commitments. The good news is that when teams apply the commitment-based approach, commitments are more and more likely to align to the top-down request date as the project progresses. The principle in action here is "success breeds success." As the team members consistently succeed at meeting their commitments, they often become bolder in setting later project commitments, and reconciliation becomes less of an issue.

Outputs from the Team Planning Meeting

The last 20 to 30 minutes of the team planning meeting are spent formalizing the meeting outcomes and making sure team members know how the plan will be used by the team to keep the project on track. When an outside facilitator is used (someone not on this project team, professional or not), he or she *should not* be responsible for capturing the outputs from the meeting. That responsibility needs to stay within the project, preferably with the project manager.

It should be clear by now that the primary output of the team planning meeting is a partial deliverables matrix. During item 9 of the agenda (wrap-up and next steps), the team should agree on steps for finalizing commitments and getting the matrix documented and distributed to all team members for validation. The matrix should contain all the deliverables from the deliverables map and commit dates for those deliverables in the designated "first horizon" of the project plan. Where appropriate, some deliverables owners may have permission to firm up their commitments in the next few days. And it should be clarified, during wrap-up, that owners of each internal deliverable in the first horizon need to complete any quality criteria conversations with their listed users that weren't completed in the meeting. (Note that the matrix doesn't show the actual quality criteria; it just tracks whether or not the owners and users have reached an agreement.) Some project managers request that quality criteria be documented and submitted to the leadership, but an effective performance system only requires that the conversations be tracked.

Also notice that only one owner is listed on the matrix for each internal deliverable. During item 5 of the team planning meeting agenda, it is important for team members to put their names on each internal deliverable to which they expect to contribute (as described in the appendix). However, for performance system purposes, all that is needed is to list the ultimate owner, and this should always be one individual. Sometimes multiple users can also be represented by their team leader. There will still be multiple users when multiple downstream internal deliverables depend upon one upstream internal deliverable.

Another likely output from the meeting is an "action item list." The action item list identifies issues that were brought up as assumptions were tested, but that the participants and ultimately the meeting driver decided needed further study before resolving (see Figure 32). Each of these issues should have an individual owner and a committed date for completion. This list will be reviewed in upcoming progress review meetings.

	Project:	Code Name "Star"			Ultimate Deliverable:		Switching System (SVR)		WW: 18	

| | Project Manager: | C. Egton | | | Customer: | AP&P Corp. | | | | |

	Item	Deliverables	Owner	User(s)	Quality Reqs	Commit Date (WW)	Done?	Comments
	1	S.P.P.	C.E.	J.P.M T.Y., T.B.	◯	◯		Holes to be Filled
	2	Market Analysis	J.P.	C.E.	Y	21		
	3	F.D.D.	T.Y.	T.B., A.L., N.B.	Y	25		
First project horizon as determined by subteams	4	S.D.D.	T.B.	T.B., N.B., B.C., F.Q., A.L.	Y	31		
	5	Arch. Spec.	T.B.	A.L., F.Q., C.E., N.B., B.C.	Y	33		
	6	P.I.D.	C.E.	C.E.	◯	◯		
	7	Feature Test Plans	N.B.	B.C., A.L., F.Q., N.B., D.J.	◯	◯		
	8	Design Spec. HW	B.C.	N.B., B.C.	Y			
	9	Design Spec. SW	A.L.	N.B., A.L.	Y			
	10	Design Spec. FW	F.Q.	N.B., F.Q.	Y			

Figure 31. Example of Deliverables Matrix with Holes That Need To Be Filled

The validated deliverables map is another meeting output. Although most of the information from it should be captured in the deliverables matrix, keeping it intact can save the team time in the next team planning meeting (to be held around the end of the first project horizon). The other meeting output is the quality requirements defined for several internal deliverables. Although some teams prefer to formalize these and get them into a word processing file, this is not necessary. The alternative is to have the owners of these deliverables take the quality criteria with them to post in the area where the work will be done. This brings up an important point about planning documentation in general. **Most of the value of the team planning meeting is not in the resulting documentation but in the conversations and commitments between team members throughout the day.** Only if these conversations are continued, frequently and in an appropriate format, can the team expect to emerge from the vicious cycle and deliver on their commitments.

Item #	Action /Desired Outcome	Owner	Commit Date	Done?
1	Test sponsors assumptions about market analysis	J.P.	WW 19	
2	Resolve "timing" issue in architecture	T.B.	WW 21	
3	Etc.			

Figure 32. Example of Action Item List

As stated at the beginning of this chapter, the commitment management approach is largely about getting the right people thinking and talking about the right things at the right time. Chapter 5 discusses regular progress review meetings, where the output of the team planning meeting becomes the basis for continuing these conversations in the form of a project-level performance system. Chapter 6 follows that up with a discussion on how the same conversations are kept alive with subteam and individual-level performance systems. Like the team planning process, each level of performance system is managed through a specific meeting format and adherence to a few simple rules (the three reporting rules).

Summary

- Building commitment to a project plan requires letting team members share and test their assumptions about the project. The team planning meeting is designed to make sure assumptions are shared as the team works through the components of a commitment-based plan.

- The main objectives of the team planning meeting are:
    — to move towards a set of mostly shared assumptions,
    — to understand and document issues that arise as assumptions are shared and tested,
    — to clarify cross-functional expectations and

— to build whole team commitment to the resulting project plan.

- Effective planning meetings require early inclusion (equal opportunity for participation from all attendees) and explicit ground rules.

- The "Dump and Clump" is a group process that allows assumptions to be shared and tested first at the small group level and then at the whole project level.

- As assumptions are tested and sorted through, decisions will need to be made. Consultative decision making encourages participation but still leads to timely decisions.

- In the initial team planning meeting, commitments are defined only for the first project horizon. It is more important to have commitment to a small part of the plan than to have a comprehensive plan based on hope and "acceptable lies."

- The way bottom-up commitments are reconciled with the top-down request date sets the tone for whether trade-offs will be revealed or concealed throughout the rest of the project.

- A step-by-step guide for facilitating the team planning meeting is provided in the appendix.

1. Rick Dehmel, conversation with author, May 1996.

2. William R. Daniels, *Group Power I: A Manager's Guide to Using Task-Force Meetings* (San Diego: Universal Associates, 1986).

3. W. R. Daniels and J. G. Mathers, *Change-ABLE Organization: Key Practices for Speed and Flexibility* (Mill Valley: ACT Publishing, 1997).

4. Harold Kerzner, *Project Management: A Systems Approach to Planning, Scheduling and Controlling*, 2nd edition (New York: Van Nostrand Reinhold Co., 1984).

5. E. M. Goldratt, *Critical Chain* (Great Barrington: The New River Press Publishing Co., 1997).

Project-Level Progress Review Meetings

Project Manager:	Will your team's prototype be done by the end of the week as scheduled?
Subteam Leader:	Are you kidding? We've spent most of this week getting ready for this afternoon's big project review!

This brief dialogue encompasses much of what's wrong with project reviews in many organizations. The most obvious problem in the scenario is that the review process has become a "resource sink." It is not uncommon on complex projects for project team members to wonder why so much time is spent collecting and reporting what they often perceive as inane data. But the scenario also hints at more subtle symptoms of a team in the vicious cycle.

First of all, to serve their purpose, progress reviews need to be frequent. "Big deal" project reviews, held at the request of project stakeholders once a quarter or every other month, won't result in timely decisions even if the right things are presented in the right way. More importantly though, if

99

team members and subteam leaders are jumping through hoops to collect the data they are supposed to present, then they are not presenting the most important information about the project. The information that is required to make sound decisions about continuing, modifying or killing a project is "performance data" and should be at team members' fingertips.

Another danger sign in this scenario is that the subteam leader did not feel compelled to tell the project manager that a key deliverable was being delayed until it was too late to do anything about it. Therefore, the team is obviously not adhering to Reporting Rule #3, which is about providing early warning as soon as a deliverable is in jeopardy of slipping. When this rule is ignored, progress reviews are often treated as a forum for analyzing how far behind the team is (and rationalizing how slips will be "made up" later) rather than as a forum for keeping the project on track in the first place.

This chapter describes a different approach to the progress review meeting. It is an approach built on the foundation of a commitment-based plan, designed to keep trade-offs overt and to keep the team informed of what they need to know and do to ensure success. In this approach, progress review meetings are a vehicle for getting the team into a performance system. These meetings use simple tools for tracking and viewing progress and for managing uncertainty (risks) and other factors not completely in the control of the project team. The final ingredients for effective progress reviews are the three rules for reporting progress:

1. Performance data simply shows whether what was committed to be done is done or not.

2. Whoever executes the plan generates the performance data that is used to make decisions.

3. Expect early warning of commitments that may be missed and never punish anyone for providing early warning.

Predicting Future Performance

Progress review meetings should not be used as a "catch all" opportunity to share information and to problem solve. They have two specific objectives. The first is determining whether or not the team is accomplishing what it committed to accomplish and, therefore, whether or not it is likely to accomplish the stated business goals. As stated in Chapter 2: **Past performance is the only reliable predictor of future performance.** [1]

Teams that are reliably meeting their commitments during the early phases of the project are much more likely to meet their commitments (both schedule and quality) in later phases. An effective performance system gives the team reliable information about whether they are meeting their commitments. Teams that are missing commitments, but telling themselves that they will catch up on later deliverables, are engaging in what one project manage-

Item	Activity	Objective	Time
1	Project manager passes down any changes to project scope or business plan.	Ensure project plan is still aligned to business plan.	0–10 min.
2	Review deliverables due this week.	Deliverable owners affirm that they have accomplished what they had committed.	3–12 min. (depends on number due)
3	Three week "look ahead"	Verify that future commitments are on track. Opportunity for deliverable owners to give early warning that they need help.	5–30 min. (depends on number coming due)
4	Review progress on high-risk deliverables.	Anticipate potential "rocks" in the plan.	3–12 min.
5	Review outcomes of action items from previous meetings.	Verify that actions assigned to prevent schedule slips and address potential problems have occurred and have accomplished what was expected.	5–20 min.

Figure 33. Project-Level Progress Review Agenda

ment expert calls "magical thinking." When there is no rational plan to explain how a team is going to catch up after missing commitments, the only way they will catch up is if "something magical" happens.

The second objective of the project level review meeting is to anticipate commitments that are in jeopardy of being missed and to ensure appropriate trade-offs are made so a commitment can be salvaged if at all possible. This is the important concept of early warning. Successful teams don't have crystal balls. They make some poor estimates and judgments just as unsuccessful teams do. However, successful teams anticipate when a poor estimate or judgment has been made rather than finding out (or revealing it) when it is too late to save the commitment. **Successful teams put their effort into preventing schedule slips rather than working overtime trying to recover from them.** Figure 33 is a review-meeting agenda designed to achieve the two stated objectives.

Managing Commitments and Risk

Passing Down Project Changes

No matter how many refinements are made to a project's definition (customer deliverables, features, performance levels, etc.), it will always be in someone's interest to "tweak" it some more. Effective project managers realize this and are willing to say "no" many times to definition changes on a project. It is also true that project definitions are rarely perfect at the outset. So project managers need to know when to "pick their battles." They need to recognize when a definition change is unavoidable, but otherwise actively protect their team from chronic additions to features and product performance (scope creep).

Almost as troublesome as scope creep are the rumors of scope creep. When rumors of potential definition changes are allowed to circulate and fester, it is common for team members to anticipate definition changes and slow down progress so that they won't "waste time focusing on the wrong features." It is the role of project leadership to shield the team from both scope creep and definition-change rumors. Team members should not consider the impact of any definition change until they are asked to do so by leadership. In fact, some project managers set strict rules about how potential definition changes will be discussed and with whom.

When the full impact of a proposed definition change has been understood (in terms of schedule, scope and resources), and the change is determined necessary and approved by the project manager, each subteam leader needs to gain a recommitment from his or her team members. The outcomes of the subteam re-commitment discussions are what need to be reviewed at the next project-level progress review. This agenda item will only be relevant when a definition change has occurred, which should be the exception rather than the rule. But it is important that the project plan get aligned to its definition (or business plan) changes immediately after they are approved.

Reviewing Deliverables Due This Week

Anyone who owns a deliverable due in the current week should be present or represented at the review meeting. These owners need to declare their due deliverables done or not done (per Reporting Rule #1). Remember that 95 percent done is *not* done. As each owner declares his or her completed deliverable, the primary user of that deliverable should be asked to confirm that he or she received the deliverable from the owner, and that the deliv-

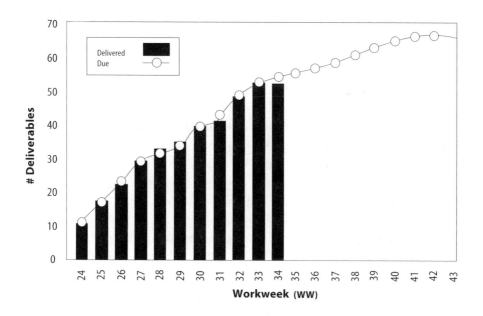

Figure 34. Example of Performance Against Commitment (PAC) Chart

erable meets the agreed to quality requirements. There should be very few surprises during this portion of the meeting if everyone has committed to Reporting Rule #3—expect early warning of commitments that may be missed—which implies commitments that are in danger of being missed must be brought to the attention of the leadership before the deliverable is due. A simple and excellent indicator of whether or not the team is following this rule is called the performance against commitment (PAC) chart. The last section of this chapter will discuss how to reinforce this rule if the team is not following it early on.

The PAC chart shows the cumulative number of deliverables due each week, according to the deliverables matrix. The cumulative number of deliverables due is compared with the cumulative number of deliverables completed through a certain week. The chart should be updated at this point in the meeting. A good rule to follow is that subteams should have completed a minimum of 90 percent of the deliverables due the week they were due. As long as the team performs at this level they will likely finish the project within about 10 percent of their committed plan, which is significantly better than most product development projects. For the most part, reviewing the PAC chart should be a positive experience. It clearly shows that the team is following through on its commitments, and the chart should be used actively and frequently by team leadership to praise and encourage team members.

The Three-Week Look Ahead
A frequent assessment of whether subteams expect to complete upcoming deliverables on time may be the most important component of the review meeting. How to assess progress on in-progress deliverables is described in Chapter 6. The review meeting simply ensures that all subteam leaders and other deliverable owners are doing frequent assessments and that potential problem areas and resulting trade-offs are made visible and addressed. Deliverable owners, who consistently have upcoming deliverables in jeopardy, will have some extra footwork to do to prepare for the review meeting. This provides a natural incentive to plan commitments more carefully in the future.

The review of upcoming deliverables should *not* be on an exception basis. The team should walk through all deliverables coming due in the next several weeks and have the owners declare whether or not each deliverable, with its

Early Warning Report

Deliverable: _____ Commit Date: _____

Owner: _____ Current Date: _____

What is done so far? _____
_____
_____
_____

Expected completion date without any trade-off: _____

Expected impact of this date: _____
_____
_____
_____

Key Assumptions: _____
_____
_____
_____
_____
_____

Recommended trade-offs and/or recovery plan: _____
_____
_____
_____

Recommit date with this trade-off: _____

Figure 35. Example of Early-Warning Report Format

expected quality requirements, is on track to finish on time. For any deliverables that are in jeopardy, the owner needs to present the factors causing the delay, the expected effect if the commitment is missed and, if possible, a specific recommendation for a trade-off that will allow the commitment to be honored. Again, possible trade-offs include changing quality requirements, adding resources from outside the subteam, asking the team to work some targeted overtime, etc. Working overtime is a trade-off because there is a limited period of time that people can work extended hours and be fully productive. If you use overtime to solve this week's problem, you are pushing your luck if you try and use it as a solution to next week's problem.

Deliverable owners should never perceive they are being punished by leadership for providing early warning of a potential problem. Early warning gives the team the opportunity to look at trade-offs from a whole project perspective and choose whether to let this specific commitment slip or to create a plan to prevent missing the commitment.

Just like commitments, recovery plans are based on a set of assumptions. It is appropriate for leadership to test those assumptions in an attempt to ensure the most appropriate trade-off regarding this deliverable. However, be careful that review meetings don't turn into meetings for solving specific subteam problems. If a proposed recovery plan needs lengthy discussion, schedule a separate meeting with just those people needed to address that recovery plan in the context of the whole project plan. One person should be responsible for coordinating that meeting and reporting progress in the next review meeting (or sooner, if appropriate). These meetings and other follow-up actions are also commitments. They should be documented in the action items list with names and due dates.

Reviewing Progress Against High-Risk Deliverables
A common practice of project teams is to rate the risk of specific deliverables or tasks. For example, each task might be assigned a number or a color (green = low, yellow = medium and red = high) indicating the risk to on-time completion. The problem with this approach is that it allows the team to confuse risk with poor execution. In this scenario, any subteam that senses it is falling behind its commitment, can simply elevate its risk factor from low to medium, etc. "Risk" becomes the measure of the likelihood that subteams will manage themselves poorly, rather than a measure of whether uncertainty is being systematically reduced.

Item #	Deliverable	Owner	Current Risk Level	Date Risk Level is Expected to Improve	Comments
15	Feature "x" coded	A.M.	2	WW36	Two potential solutions
24	Thermal solution	B.C.	3	No commit yet	
43	Final test	T.L.	3	No commit yet	

From deliverables matrix

Risk Level Definitions:
Level
3 Risk   = Solution not known
2 Risk   = One or more potential solutions being evaluated
1 Risk   = Solution approved and being implemented
0 No Risk = Solution successfully implemented

Figure 36. Example Risk Matrix and Definitions of Risk Levels

For our purposes we will define risk as *the probability of not finding a solution to a problem that must be resolved in order for the project to succeed.* Therefore, a deliverable that involves a problem with no clear solution is a high-risk deliverable. By this definition, deliverables with risk should be significantly fewer, and this risk will primarily have to do with technology and methodology. For example, when the first videoconferencing products were being developed, it became apparent to developers in the industry that integrated services data networks (ISDN) would provide the best video interface, but the technology was new and it wasn't clear it would even be available for users. Rather than wait until ISDN was determined viable (or not), one company began development and simultaneously pursued three alternative porting strategies. When the decision was eventually made to go with ISDN, the product was largely ready for implementation (had the decision gone another way, the team also would have been ready).

Figure 36 operationally defines three specific risk levels, but some teams get even more specific within these three levels. For example, one team divided level 2 into two levels of risk based on the amount and nature of the evaluation data collected to date. The point is that the team should use common and specific definitions.

A *risk matrix* can be integrated into the deliverables matrix or kept separate. The risk matrix makes sure that deliverables involving substantial risk are reviewed throughout the project rather than just three weeks before they are due. It should indicate the current level of risk (per the given definitions) for those deliverables where the definition applies. It should also indicate a committed date for when the risk is expected to move to the next lower level. In the example provided, deliverable number 15 should move from level 2 to level 1 risk in workweek 36. This means the owners of deliverable 15 expect to evaluate alternative solutions by that date.

These commit dates should be treated just like the others on the deliverables matrix. The commitments must be made by the people doing the work, and they should be held to the same ground rules (e.g. done or not done and early warning if there is any danger of not finishing on time). When this approach to classifying and tracking risk is followed, risk becomes useful information rather than a source of chronic concern and ambiguity.

Review Outcomes of Action Items
At the end of each review meeting the team should look at the actions assigned in previous review meetings that were scheduled to be completed. Again, be careful not to let this section of the meeting turn into problem solving. The only issue to be discussed here is whether the items planned to be resolved by now have been resolved. And if not, decide when they will be resolved. If issues have arisen requiring discussion, separate meetings should be set up with the appropriate owners and/or subteams. As a general rule, review meetings should be kept separate from planning and problem-solving meetings.[2] When this rule is followed, review meetings are relatively crisp and short and provide a clear picture of whether the team is performing according to its plan and, therefore, whether it is likely to maintain this performance in the future.

Effective Meetings
It is important that progress review meetings be crisp and relatively short because they are needed frequently in order to keep projects on track. At the beginning of a project, just after the initial team-planning meeting, it is recommended that teams review their progress weekly. At certain key points in the project, progress reviews may be needed twice a week or even daily. In the middle of a project phase, if things are going exceptionally well, project level progress reviews might be cut back to twice a month. It is not

recommended having them any less frequently than that.

Established meeting behaviors do not change over night. One way to speed up the transition to more effective progress reviews is to have someone observe and provide coaching in these meetings until new behaviors have been learned. Coaches need to be someone without a role or stake in the actual project.

CASE STUDY

Information Technology (IT) Projects: A Special Case?

The Challenge

Ask product development managers what makes their projects especially challenging and many will say it is the need to hit market windows. Project managers in the competitive bidding environment will argue that they have it worse than product developers because their delivery dates are driven by a predetermined contract. So it's not surprising that when a successful IT project manager (Helen) was asked what makes IT projects so challenging, she said, "IT projects *really do* have finite timeframes because projects are constrained by financial and other information system freezes." Although real deadlines probably are not the key difference of IT projects, these projects do have some unique challenges.

One major challenge is that IT projects usually have multiple sponsors and often as many project objectives as there are system users. The IT sponsors have to worry about large-scale system compatibility and maintainability. The business sponsors and system users are usually most concerned about a seamless transition (to a new, upgraded or converted system) and specific new functionality. In the early stages of an IT project, it often *seems* prudent to gloss over some of these scope conflicts and just get something going. But leaving these issues unresolved is like setting sail in whatever way the wind is blowing before clarifying your destination.

Another challenge of IT projects is that the contributors to the project are often highly distributed. Geographical distribution is a challenge in many project environments, but IT project contributors are also often distributed organizationally. Many corporate IT projects literally impact every organization in the company (both profit and loss and cost centers). This means IT project teams are really just a loose conglomeration of folks that have some sort of interest in the system in question. Not exactly a rallying cry for teamwork!

So what are the implications for those lucky enough to be IT project managers? About six months ago, Helen completed what she considers one of her most successful IT projects to date. It was an upgrade to an existing administrative system that was in the critical path of a larger strategic system implementation. Helen and her comanager were given a deadline (dictated by the larger implementation) and the resources to assemble a core team of the system users face to face one time for five days. (They were distributed across more than twenty-five geographical locations around the world.)

The Results
The face-to-face team meeting occurred in April. The drop-dead date for full conversion was November 16th, but the team was asked to complete it by October 19th to provide some buffer. The successful conversion was completed on October 19th as planned. The PAC chart showed that the team had accomplished 88 percent of their deliverables on or before their committed date, and the ones that slipped were rapidly recovered. Although IT project teams are often rife with finger pointing, according to the postmortem

report, "The core team of 30 project contributors agreed, to a person, that this was the best IT project they had participated on." Two hundred and fifty overall contributors were included in the celebration of success.

Planned Rework

It was a smooth project, but not without unexpected hitches. After the team had set their system "freeze" date (indicating no more system changes before conversion) for the beginning of May, they were told they would have to accommodate changes to another system through the end of June. The team came up with the creative solution of "planned rework." Rather than try and accommodate each change as it occurred, the changes in May and June were ignored by the team but meticulously tracked. When they had the system meeting their own standards, they dealt with the changes just as they would have dealt with rework. Thanks to predetermined internal deliverable quality criteria, there was minimal unplanned rework to speak of.

How the Results Were Achieved

A great deal of effort was focused on getting consensus from all sponsors on the project goals and measures of success before assembling the core team. The first two days of the core team's face-to-face meeting were spent getting to know one another and getting buy-in to the project goals. Much of the next two days were spent following the "team planning meeting" format as described in Chapters 3 and 4. Helen also set aside a day to prioritize the system enhancement requests, which she knew the users would bring to the meeting. However, after agreeing on the project goals, and participating in the plan to achieve those goal, the users unanimously agreed that a long list of enhancements would put the overall project goals in jeopardy. Enhancements were put on hold until it was clear the primary goal was under control.

Helen was coming off another IT project where a couple of "key players" had been tasked with drafting the project plan and loading it into a software program that would assist ongoing management of the project. In her opinion, the automated plan was never bought into by the rest of the team and, as a result, people complained throughout about spending all their time updating a "bogus" schedule.

On this project, Helen decided to take a simpler approach, using the deliverables matrix and PAC chart almost exclusively for project tracking and reporting. The approach was presented at the end of the team planning meeting, and team members were asked to buy into Reporting Rule #3 (the early warning rule). Helen believes this buy-in was important because most of the slipped milestones were by individuals that had not been able to make the face-to-face meeting. However, the response to all slips was the same. Focus was put on understanding and resolving the issues rather than placing blame.

The global core team met by phone every week and used the deliverables matrix to track actual progress and to look ahead two weeks at a time. Helen used the PAC chart both with the team and for reporting to her IT steering committee. According to Helen, "The steering committee liked the PAC chart format so well, it became the reporting standard for the other projects going on at the same time."

Are IT projects a special case? In some ways they probably are. What's the best way to ensure excellent execution? Helen would say commitment-based planning and tracking.

Dealing with "Bad News"

There are essentially three types of bad news that can emerge while a team is reviewing progress against its committed plan. The first type emerges during the "look ahead" section of the meeting. If early warnings are happening for 0-20 percent of the deliverables reviewed so far, what might seem like bad news really isn't bad news at all. As long as the other 80 percent are meeting their commitments, and as long as the 20 percent are providing early warning with thoughtful recovery plans, your team is not operating in the vicious cycle. Encourage the current level of performance, hold owners accountable for meeting their approved recovery plans and press on.

When recovery plans are needed for more than 20 percent of the deliverables reviewed to date, you may learn that the team needs to improve its ability to make commitments. One of the fastest ways to improve planning and estimating skills is to make sure the team reviews its progress-versus-plans frequently, as has just been described. If lots of early warnings persist, it may be necessary to ask the teams to revisit their commitments and give them an opportunity to adjust them *this one time*. When this is the case, it is recommended that the performance-against-commitment progress to date be carried forward, but after future commitments have been adjusted, the "cumulative deliverables due" section of the PAC chart should be adjusted to reflect the new commit dates. If PAC performance does not immediately improve to 90 percent or better after such an adjustment, then something other than planning and estimating is the problem.

A more serious problem is when commitments are slipping, without early warning, in the week they are due. It may take a couple of incidents to get the new reporting rules to sink in, but before long, missed commits without warning should be near zero. When that is not the case, team members involved are not taking their commitments seriously and viewing them as personal promises. Under these circumstances, the project manager needs to find out why this is the case. There are a variety of ways to do this, but they all involve talking with team members (one on one, in small groups or as an entire team) in an environment where they are encouraged to be completely honest (and without repercussions or judgments by management).

Teams that have been operating in the vicious cycle in the past may not yet be convinced that project leadership really wants to know how long they think things will take, or that they really want to know when things are not going as planned. The role of the project manager here is to convince the team that following Reporting Rule #3 (providing early warning) is much more important than trying to "make things look good" for management. Find out if anyone feels that they have already been punished or discouraged for being honest about the project. If so, then the leadership team has some work to do on its own behavior before reinforcing the reporting rules with the team. If and when the team members choose to hold themselves accountable, it is absolutely imperative that leadership lives up to its part of Reporting Rule #3 (never punish anyone for providing early warning)!

Teams that cannot work through this issue, and neglect to begin taking individual responsibility for commitments (both making good ones and meeting them), are doomed to vicious-cycle levels of performance and morale. That is the choice the team is making in this situation. This level of "soul-searching" may require some help from skilled and objective facilitators.

The third type of bad news that arises in the review meeting is that one or more risk areas is turning out much worse than expected. This type of bad news is sort of a two-edged sword. On the one hand, now that the team is invested in the project, it is possible that this type of challenge will cause a breakthrough innovation—a new solution to the problem that has a positive impact on the total project plan. On the other hand, risks mean that there is a chance of failure. Therefore, it is important that leadership be supportive when a risk area starts looking bad. By making the problem visible early, the owners of the risk area are doing their job, and they shouldn't be punished for being bearers of bad news. As soon as the issues are well understood, the project team needs to inform the project sponsors that the plan will be changing significantly. In the absence of a breakthrough innovation, there is a possibility that when the sponsors understand the impact of the change, they will determine the project is no longer feasible from a business standpoint. From the overall organization's perspective, this is much better than continuing the project in the hope that a miracle will happen and sinking more and more resources into a lost cause. If the decision is to move forward, and the changes have an impact on many of the project deliverables, it is possible that a full team planning meeting will be warranted to reestablish and recommit to the project plan. However the plan is revised, getting commitment from the affected team members must be involved.

One more note about failure. **Teams that manage their commitments well haven't failed just because it turns out that their project needs to be cancelled for business reasons.** It is beneficial to the entire organization when imprudent projects are cancelled sooner rather than later. When teams are operating in the vicious cycle, imprudent projects often drag on months after many members of the team can tell that the projects objectives are in significant jeopardy. These projects are wasting (and demoralizing) valuable human assets that would be much better utilized on other more viable projects.

A PAC chart that shows that the team was meeting its commitments up until the decision to cancel the project is something that the team can be proud of. Achieving a project's desired business goals is never completely in the control of any member of the project team. What they can control is meeting their own commitments consistently and providing ample warning when things go wrong. If they do so, the sense of control and satisfaction that come with having things under control will exist even on projects that don't make it to completion. This allows team members to approach their new assignment with a sense of pride rather than with shame or grief.

Other Review Considerations

Just as in the scenario at the beginning of the chapter, it is common in many organizations for project teams to periodically hold a project review where the project sponsors and stakeholders attend to be informed and ask questions of team members first hand. Because sponsors and other stakeholders bring their own assumptions and perspectives, the potential exists to get useful new ideas and information surfaced in these meetings. At the same time, project reviews without the proper expectations and structure can become an unnecessary and even morale damaging experience for the project team. Chapter 7 provides advice on what sponsors and stakeholders should be looking for in these reviews to make good business decisions. When it is apparent that these reviews are not going to be structured that way, the project leadership should try and reduce the frequency of these meetings (while continuing the team's weekly progress reviews) and minimize the impact on the team members.

One way these meetings can damage morale is if team members are sent the message that they have failed if they miss the top-down request date for the project, even if they meet all of their commitments. Project leadership may need to get creative to prevent this from happening. One approach is to agree to some ground rules for the meeting ahead of time with the sponsors and stakeholders. Another approach is to prepare the team members for what they are likely to hear, and then get them focused back on the team's commitments as soon as possible after the review.

It is in everyone's best interests that every internal deliverable be delivered on the committed date, with the quality specified. This chapter discussed how to know if that is how your project is performing, and to some extent, what to do if it is not. Chapter 6 offers a proactive tool for increasing the chances that individuals, subteams and, hence, the overall team will meet their commitments. It can also be used as a response when one or more subteams struggle to meet their commitments. Once again, the answer is performance systems and, once again, they are organized in meetings, but on a smaller scale.

Summary

- A commitment-based plan lays the foundation for turning progress reviews into an effective performance system.

- The two objectives of progress reviews are to:
    1. determine if the team is accomplishing what it planned to accomplish and
    2. anticipate any deliverable commitments that are in jeopardy and make sound and timely trade-off decisions.

- For timely decision making, project-level progress reviews should be held, on average, at least weekly.

- The key components of effective progress review meetings are:
    — information passdowns (especially anything that has an impact on project scope),
    — review of deliverables due this week,
    — review of deliverables coming due in the next three weeks,
    — review of deliverables on the risk matrix and
    — review of the action item list.

- The key reporting tools used in project-level progress reviews are:
    — the deliverables matrix,
    — early-warning reports,
    — the risk matrix and
    — the action item list.

- The three reporting rules are:
    1. Performance data simply shows whether what was

committed to be done is done or not.

2. Whoever executes the plan generates the performance data that is used to make decisions.

3. Expect early warning of commitments that may be missed and never punish anyone for providing early warning.

■ Teams that have reliably met their commitments should be considered successful, even if the appropriate business decision was to cancel the project before completion. Timely cancellation of an imprudent project has a positive impact on an organization's overall success.

1. Thomas F. Gilbert, *Human Competence: Engineering Worthy Performance*, Tribute Edition (Washington DC: The International Society of Performance Improvement, 1996).

2. William R. Daniels, *Group Power II: A Manager's Guide to Conducting Regular Meetings* (San Diego: Pfeiffer & Co., 1990).

Subteam-Level Progress Review Meetings

When teams set up the performance system described in Chapter 5 and start to consistently meet their commitments, team members will become more intent than ever about meeting their project plan and the business goals. However, positive intent is not always sufficient to ensure success. Just as the project manager and subteam leader need reliable information about whether subteams are performing according to their deliverable commits, subteam members need reliable information about where they stand regarding their commitment to deliver something three weeks, eight weeks, even twenty or more weeks from now. In other words, each subteam needs to operate with its own performance system.

Structured correctly, regular subteam progress review meetings can become the basis for subteam and individual performance systems, just as the project-level progress review forms the basis for the whole project performance system. Ideally, the subteam and whole project progress reviews are coordinated so that project-level decisions are always being based on accurate and timely performance data. Each three-week look-ahead report at the

119

project level should be based on current information from a subteam level performance system.

Effective subteam performance systems require that each member of the subteam be working in a performance system. This chapter identifies the three conditions that make up individual performance systems and how to get team members working in those conditions. A variety of examples tailored to different types of work will be provided, along with instructions for developing and implementing the systems.

Subteam level performance systems can (and should) also provide the basis for continuous improvement of performance. When subteams identify and use performance data to justify improvements, they develop a sense of control over what they need to be successful. When subteams master this aspect of performance systems, they will largely manage themselves. This chapter will also describe using performance data to continuously improve.

Teams that have worked in a vicious cycle environment (even a relatively mild one) usually have some implicit or explicit habits that run counter to effective performance systems. This chapter will also discuss the possible pitfalls when implementing individual and subteam performance systems and how to overcome them. The most important mindset shift for implementing these systems is the shift from *management information systems* to *performer information systems*. This distinction will be clarified before describing how to develop your own individual and subteam performance systems.

Management Information Systems

There is an important lesson about information systems that is easiest to understand in the context of manufacturing. Consider the following true story. A trainer providing training support to a semiconductor manufacturing plant was asked to train all the manufacturing operators on a new shop-floor tracking system. The system was used to track the status and location of work in process. The training was implemented. But about three months later, the trainer was told that physical audits had determined that the operators were not entering data into the system correctly. He was asked to retrain all the operators, and being a member of a support organization, he did as he was asked. However, when he was instructed to retrain them again six months later, he began asking questions. For example, "How do we know they don't know how to enter data correctly?" "Because the data in the system is only about 65 percent accurate," they replied.

The trainer was pretty confident that training was not the issue, so he asked a couple of manufacturing supervisors to join him in a random survey of data entry skills. They went into the factory and asked operators to show them how to enter data. The operators did what they asked with almost perfect accuracy. Knowing how to correctly enter the data was not the problem. Apparently, workers were choosing not to enter data that was complete and accurate, but why?

Part of the value of an accurate shop-floor tracking system is that it can be used to identify and address the loss of in-process product. Product-loss reports were generated by the system, and beginning with the most serious losses, management would investigate where and how product was lost (made unfit for further processing). This factory was running three or four different processes and hundreds of different products at a time. Each product went through 70 to 100 process steps before it was ready to be shipped. Many of these process steps pushed the limits of current technology. And yet with all these complexities, the first step of the loss investigation process was to single out *the* responsible manufacturing worker.

Unfortunately, this is often the case with management information systems. The information is used (or perceived by the operators to be used) at least partially to assign blame or to determine some sort of differential treatment of the performers (e.g., in performance appraisals). The more accurate the information in these systems, the easier it is to place blame and label "marginal" performers. This sheds some light on the behavior of the performers.

In fact, finding out who was present when something went wrong is an important part of improving performance. Those people present when problems occur usually have valuable information that can help prevent the problem from occurring in the future. But why would anyone speak up when they risk being blamed for a problem that probably has multiple causes? As the data showed, the operators were choosing not to take that chance when they could avoid it.

This syndrome of mistreated and inaccurate management information systems is not limited to manufacturing. The chipset case in Chapter 1 revealed that the project schedule had become the same sort of management information system. Individuals and subteams would pump inaccurate information into the schedule tracking system and everyone would pretend like everything was just fine, until it was time to deliver a major tangible deliverable. Those that spoke up early, and suggested that the schedule might not be realistic, were ignored or blamed for not working hard enough. Projects consistently slipped 30 to 50 percent from the schedule.

Performer Information Systems

As long as manufacturing operators or project team members believe that reporting accurate data is likely to be used against them in some way, information systems will remain less than accurate.[1] The alternative is quite simple. Assume that performers are just as concerned about successful performance as management is. Engage the performers in using the information themselves to investigate problems and potential improvements. This makes the information system safe for them and more likely to yield performance improvements.

For organizations that have misused information systems, convincing performers that the information system is now safe (blame free) will require sending extremely clear signals about the blame-free process. A simple way to do that is to set up systems in which the information is both generated by, and "owned" by, the performers. Management can look at the information generated by these systems, but they can't use it to evaluate individual performance. It belongs to the performers and is primarily for their own use. This may in fact be the only way to restore performer confidence in management information systems, which is the only way they will ever be accurate.

Performers don't just need information about problems. Foremost, they need reliable and frequent information about whether they are on track to meet their goals. In fact, the best way to ensure that a subteam will meet its commitments is to structure subteam progress reviews to make sure each individual on the team is operating with his or her own performer information system.

The three conditions for successful performance are:

1. when individuals know exactly what they need to accomplish to be successful;

2. when individuals have frequent and reliable feedback about whether they are accomplishing it and

3. when individuals believe that if it is determined they need something to be successful, it will be provided (or the accomplishment required for success will be adjusted).

Individuals will perform successfully when they meet the three conditions for successful performance.[2,3] William Daniels, cofounder and senior consultant at American Consulting and Training, summarizes these three conditions as clear expectations, frequent feedback and control of resources, and demonstrates that people working in all three conditions are ensured of success.[4] You may have already figured out that a performer information system is the same thing as the performance system introduced in Chapter 2 and, essentially, just another version of what was described at the team level in Chapter 5.

Anatomy of an Individual Performance System

Individual and subteam-level performance systems can take a variety of forms, depending on the nature of the deliverables being produced (and, hence, the work being performed). The following example will demonstrate how an individual performance system was used on a simple one-person project to set up the three conditions for successful performance.

Amar supervised a small group of programmers that developed software to automate production equipment. The software prevented people from making simple data entry errors that could cause catastrophic losses of product. It was easiest to have one programmer create the software for each different piece of equipment. Programmers were for the most part dedicated to a piece of equipment until the program was up and running and then they would take on a new project.

Before implementing individual performance systems, Amar's programmers typically averaged eight to nine weeks to produce and implement one of these programs. But their schedules typically said they'd be done in six weeks. This meant they were slipping their schedules about 30 to 50 percent, on average. The first time Amar helped one of his programmers implement an individual performance system, her program was promised in six weeks as usual, but was implemented in six weeks and two days—a schedule slip of about 7 percent instead of 30 to 50 percent.

Here is how the system was developed. Amar and his programmer (we'll call her Sue) met in the cafeteria to plan out the next project. First, they agreed on the ultimate outcome of the project—a software program to automate a specific piece of manufacturing equipment. They agreed upon some quality criteria for the program such as writing the program in a given language, achieving an acceptable level of system reliability, using a modular approach (object-oriented programming) and providing appropriate documentation.

Next, Amar asked Sue, "What do you expect to get done on the program this week?" Since she was doing object-oriented programming, she said she would complete two "objects" in the first week. Amar then asked how many total objects would be involved in the program. Sue made a list of all the objects required, which totaled fourteen. To program fourteen objects in six weeks, they figured that she needed to produce between two and three objects per week, on average. Amar then asked, "How will you know that each object is done and done well?" Sue listed a few quality requirements that would be the criteria for completing an object.

Amar sketched a calendar of six weeks on a napkin and asked Sue to forecast when each object would be done to the defined quality requirements (see Figure 37, Sue's Project Calendar). Amar then asked Sue to post the napkin in her cubicle where he could see it. He asked that she cross out each numbered object on the napkin each time she completed that object.

Amar stopped by Sue's cubicle a couple times during the first week. When he saw the first object was done on time, he praised Sue for staying on schedule. He praised her again when she had completed both objects by the end of the first week. During the second week, Sue fell behind. Amar stopped by, but when he saw she was behind, he didn't say anything about her

Week	Monday	Tuesday	Wednesday	Thursday	Friday
1			Object 1		Object 2 Object 3
2		Object 4		Object 5	
3					Object 6
4					Object 7 Object 10
5	Object 8		Object 9 Object 10		Object 12
6					Integration & Installation

Figure 37. Sue's Project Calendar

progress. She was on schedule again by Monday. She had come in over the weekend to catch up.

During the third week she fell behind again. This time she approached Amar and said she was having trouble keeping up. Amar asked how he could help. Sue asked to be relieved from all scheduled meetings, but Amar tested her assumption that it was planned meetings that were slowing her down. Eventually they decided that unplanned interruptions were as much or more of an impact than the planned ones. Sue needed uninterrupted blocks of time to concentrate. Unfortunately, her cubicle was surrounded by other employees that were often in need of advice regarding their computer work-stations. "Why call a stranger on the phone and wait on hold," these people figured, "when the person around the corner or across the hall is an expert on computers?" To address these interruptions, they decided to hang a "Do Not Disturb" sign across Sue's cubicle entrance.

The sign was reasonably effective, and Sue found it easier to stay on schedule. She also discovered that her original estimate of six weeks was pretty aggressive. She was much better forecasting what she could accomplish in the next week or two, than three or more weeks out. Amar let her be excused from some meetings and she finished and implemented the program midway through the seventh week. Based on this outcome, all of Amar's programmers started using individual performance systems. They weren't all exactly the same, but they all improved performance significantly. Another observation of Amar's was that a couple of his most experienced programmers had already been using performance systems, only they kept them in their heads. They revisited their project plans each week and decided what they needed to accomplish without really documenting it. Amar asked them to start documenting their plans so that they could role model effective planning for the less experienced members of the group.

Amar's example offers several useful lessons for designing and implementing your own subteam and individual performance systems.

- The clearest expectations involve breaking internal deliverables into modular *subdeliverables* rather than listing sequential tasks. You can't get much clearer than an expectation to produce X number of specific subdeliverables that meet specified quality criteria by the end of this week. And when individual commitments are not this clear, subteam commitments will always be at risk of failure due to misunderstandings.

- Although the napkin on the cubicle wall told Sue if she was being successful, she still appreciated having Amar let her know that *he knew* she was being successful. An important component of the system is frequent encouragement from leadership (or even peers on a mature team).

- It is difficult to forecast your own accomplishments more than about two weeks in advance. Final deliverable goals need to be revisited every week or so and turned into commitments. In this case, Sue tried to meet a plan set six weeks in advance and ran into some difficulty. **Having control of resources isn't always about adding resources; it is often about finding ways to become efficient enough to meet your own commitments.** Sue accomplished this by reducing distractions so she would have blocks of time to concentrate. In the end she also negotiated herself out of some meetings for a short period of time to stay close to her six-week schedule.

- Successful performers often already use the three conditions to their advantage. Having them do it explicitly can have a positive influence on less successful coperformers.

Amar and Sue's example is the second smaller scale performance system described in this book. In Chapter 1, Ted's design subteam divided some of their key project deliverables (internal deliverables from the plan template) into subdeliverables and created a subteam-level performance system. Notice that several of the lessons listed apply to both of these examples. Especially lesson number one, the concept of dividing internal deliverables into modular subdeliverables. The advantage of tracking subdeliverables (versus sequential tasks) is that a pace goal can be established. The pace goal is the number of subdeliverables per person per period (usually per week) required to make a larger commitment (milestone or overall project). Individual performance to date against the pace goal tells team members if they are on pace to meet the overall subteam's commitment.[5] For example, the design engineers determined that to meet their commitment they needed to average three sub-blocks per person per week. Sue knew she needed to complete a little more than two objects per week on average.

Having a pace goal is the key to early warning on longer-term commitments. If you need to complete five subdeliverables per week to stay on pace, and find you are completing only three per week after several weeks, you know that something probably needs to be changed if you are to be successful. Sometimes when this occurs, someone comes up with a creative idea to catch up to the pace goal. If not, then a trade-off is in order, and this needs to be brought to the attention of the interested parties (supervisor and/or project leadership).

Deliverable	Modular Subdeliverables
Object-Oriented Program	Objects programmed per week
Computer Chip Specification	Sub-blocks documented per week
Computer Chip Model	Sub-blocks coded per week
Computer Chip Test Bank	Tests written per week
Book	Pages written per week
Sales	New prospects per week and design wins per month
Process Problem Solved	Fishbones ruled out per week (see next example)

Figure 38. Deliverables and Modular Subdeliverables

When team members are first introduced to individual or subteam-level performance systems they are often resistant to the idea that their work can be neatly modularized. They will often say, "Our work is too unpredictable." or "I do creative work and you can't plan out creative work." There are some kinds of work that are very difficult to modularize, but individuals and teams that decide to try performance systems often use their creativity to come up with a way to accomplish this task. Each module does not have to be the same or even very similar. What is critical is that the sum of all the modules equals the larger deliverable, and that each subdeliverable represents what one person can do in one week or less. Figure 38 is a list of example deliverables and the modularized subdeliverables that have been used to track them.

The last example is an extremely creative example of modularizing a deliverable. A process development team was trying to isolate the cause and then fix a cracking problem in a new material. This team created a fishbone diagram of possible causes and then set individual goals around ruling out specific fishbones. The problem, which had plagued this team for the previous three months, was eliminated in two weeks.

Sub-Deliverable Report for WW: 18   Team Member: Nancy King

Next weeks subdeliverables	Status
1. Complete assignments from Integration meeting	
2. Verify Section D test coverage vs. Test plan	
3. Risk report for hi-val solution	
4. Inputs to Section H team	
5. Self study module for new workstation	
6. Commitment from H team for sync date	
7. Half day off	

This weeks subdeliverables	Status
1. Section D test ready	Done
2. Inputs to G team	Done
3. Test plan comprehended	Done
4. Complete assignments from Integration meeting	Not done
5. Intern has goals for next week	Done

Figure 39. Example of Individual-Level Tracking Without Modular Subdeliverables

In the event that your team decides there is just no way to modularize its work, there is still substantial benefit to implementing performance systems. Figure 39 is an example of this type of individual performance system. Instead of forecasting X number of subdeliverables per week, individuals can forecast each of the key tasks he or she will complete in a given week. Even in this example, note that most of the items are stated in terms of subdeliverables rather than tasks. It is more difficult to tell if the individual or team is on pace in this example; however, the system still reveals if individuals are reliably meeting their own commitments each week. If they are not doing so, then it is likely that the larger commitment is also in jeopardy. This type of performance system should still increase the productivity of any individual not already working in a performance system.[6]

Six Steps to Developing Subteam-Level Performance Systems

1. Define the Final Deliverable

This is the final deliverable for a specific performance system. In Sue's case, her individual performance system applied to her entire project. Her final deliverable was the overall project deliverable—an installed equipment automation program. On a complex project, the final deliverable of an individual or subteam performance system will be one of the project's internal deliverables from the deliverables matrix. For example, the final deliverable of the subteam performance system in Chapter 1 was an architecture specification document. When the design team delivered the architecture specification, they modified their performance system around their next major deliverable (i.e., the chip model). Not every deliverable on the project will need it's own performance system, but labor-intensive deliverables (those that will take one or more people more than two or three weeks to complete) will. The design of the subteam-level performance system needs to be revisited for each new subteam deliverable.

2. List Modular Subdeliverables (if possible)

The advantage of breaking the final deliverable into modular subdeliverables was just described. This is the part of developing a subteam-level performance system that often takes some creativity. How can the final deliverable be broken down into modules—relatively uniform subdeliverables—that one performer can complete in one week or less? Circuit board and integrated circuit design can often be broken down into functional sections of the circuit board or silicon chip. Amar and his programmer broke their object-oriented automation program down into discrete program "objects." Documents can be broken into chapters, or sections or pages. Remember that it is not necessary that each subdeliverable be exactly the same or even take the same amount of time or effort to produce. As long as they each take one week or less to produce, they will serve the purpose of the performance system. Any inequities in time and effort required will be dealt with in the last step of developing your performance system.

If the subteam leader and performers are unable to come up with a modular breakdown of the final deliverable, skip the next two steps.

3. Define Quality Requirements for Subdeliverables

Remember the goal here is a clear performance expectation. To accomplish this, there must be explicit quality requirements. Each performer needs to know he or she has only completed a subdeliverable when all quality criteria have been met. This is also part of a performer's frequent performance feedback, so quality requirements need to be such that the performer can self-determine if they have been met immediately after completing the subdeliverable. This usually means a practical limit of two to three quality criteria, and they will be the same ones for each subdeliverable. The subdeliverable quality criteria can usually be derived from the deliverable quality criteria generated in the team planning meeting. Just as with deliverable quality requirements at the project level, the key question is, "How will we know when each subdeliverable is done and done well?"

4. Determine the Pace Goal

The pace goal is most often defined as output per week. In this case, take the total number of subdeliverables required to produce the final deliverable (sometimes this is an estimate) and divide that number by the number of weeks to the committed delivery date for the final deliverable. This is the average required output per week. If this is a subteam performance system, divide this number by the number of performers working on the final deliverable. This number is the average required output per week, per person, which is the "pace goal." Amar's programmer's pace goal was a little over two objects per week. In Chapter 1, the design team knew exactly how many sub-blocks per week per person were needed to stay on its pace goal.

Individual Tracking Sheet

Developer: K. Poret

Test Name	Commit Date	Coded By	Done	Documented By	Done	In Bank By	Done
A sub	WW18	Monday	✓	Tuesday	✓	Tuesday	✓
A sweep	WW18	Thursday	✓	Friday	✓	Friday	✓
A time	WW19	Monday	✓	Monday	✓	Monday	✓
A blast	WW19	Wednesday		Thursday		Thursday	
A farm	WW19	Thursday		Friday		Friday	
B sub							
B sweep							

Figure 40. Example of Individual Tracking of Modular Subdeliverables (Tracking Test Writing)

5. Define How Completed Subdeliverables are Tracked

Ideally, each performer will have a simple performance tracking system that tells him at a glance whether he is on track to hit his personal commitment for the week. An example is the calendar that Amar and his programmer produced on the napkin. Sue knew which day each object was to be completed, and she would mark whether the object was done or not. More examples (Figures 40 and 41) are provided to give you some ideas about personal tracking systems.

The team may already have a project-wide system in place to track short-term individual progress (e.g. project tracking software). However, if this system has ever been used as a management information system, it will probably not serve the purpose desired here. The best individual tracking systems are usually on a piece of paper or a white board at the individual's primary workstation. When subdeliverables have been modularized, these tracking systems are usually in the form of a simple matrix or calendar. When subdeliverables are not modularized, they usually take the form of a "To Do" list or procedural checklist. In this case, remember to encourage the performers to list deliverables rather than tasks wherever possible.

Tracking New Materials Experiments

Experiment Checklist

Technician: _____ Current date: _____ Commit date: _____

Project Name: _____ Responsible Engineer: _____

Part Name: _____

Material Composition:

Experiment Objective:

Conclusions:

Check as completed:

Units Tested	A	B	C	Tests D	E	F	G	Complete
1	✓	✓	✓	✓	✓	✓	✓	✓
2	✓	✓	✓	✓				
3	✓	✓	✓	✓	✓	✓		
4	✓	✓	✓	✓				
5								
6								
7								
8								

Figure 41. Example of Individual Tracking of Modular Subdeliverables (Tracking Experiments)

When subdeliverables have been modularized, subteams can track the aggregate subteam progress and post it in a conspicuous place where team members will see it frequently. Ted's list for tracking sub-blocks of a chip in Chapter 1 is an example of this. Two more examples (Figures 42 and 43) are provided on following pages. Don't forget that the entire purpose of these tracking tools is to keep each performer informed about how he or she is doing compared to his or her commitments. Never let the information from these tools be used to single out individual performers or punish the subteam members in any way.

6. Define How Individuals Make Short-Term Commitments

Although the pace goal provides average output required, it is still necessary to have each individual performer commit to the specific subdeliverables they will complete each week. Remember the "acceptable lie" from the case study in Chapter 1. When performers ask what is the highest priority and

Switching System Software Development

D-team   Internal Deliverable Commit: WW25

Item	Subsection D Modules	I/O	Logic	Lay	Timing	Module Completion Date
1	DbX	Done	Done	Done	Done	WW19
2	Dload	Done	Shea -WW23	Done	Kunmar -WW25	
3	Dflong	Done	Done	Done	Done	WW20
4	Dsignd	Done	Done	Done	Done	WW20
5	Dlatch1	Done	Done	Done	Shea -WW24	
6	Dlatch0	Done	Done	Allen-WW23	Allan-WW24	
.	.	.	.	.	.	
.	.		.	.	.	
.	.	.	.	.	.	
28	Dtragn	Kumar-WW23	Nanc -WW24	Nanc -WW24	Allan-WW25	
Totals	**31**	**29/31**	**24/31**	**23/31**	**14/31**	

Figure 42. Example of Subteam-Level Tracking with Modular Subdeliverables (Tracking Software Development)

are told "everything needs to get done," they will inevitably promise to "do the best they can." Performers "doing the best they can" have no baseline against which to monitor their own progress. Some subdeliverables may be twice as complex as others, and some may involve some special issue that will take up time. Performers need to consider the pace goal, where the team stands against the pace goal so far and the specific subdeliverables they are working on this week in order to set meaningful personal commitments to which they can monitor their own performance.

This is where subteam progress reviews come in as a structure for maintaining individual and subteam-level performance systems. Once a week, subteam members should meet and report on their performance to last week's commitment and declare what they commit to accomplish in the current week. If the performance system is set up properly, each individual will be following the three reporting rules:

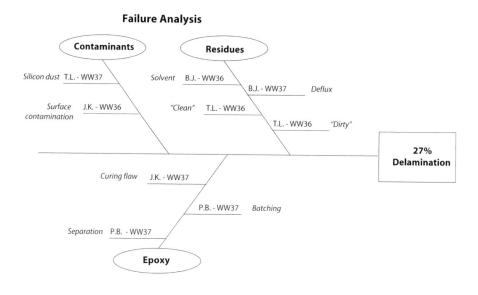

Figure 43. Example of Subteam-Level Tracking with Modular Subdeliverables (Tracking Failure Analysis—Fishbones Analyzed)

1. Performance data simply shows whether what was committed to be done is done or not.

2. Whoever executes the plan generates the performance data that is used to make decisions.

3. Expect early warning of commitments that may be missed and never punish anyone for providing early warning.

Subteam progress review meetings should be short and crisp. As with the project team-level meetings, don't let them turn into problem solving meetings. Daniels recommends holding these meetings standing up.[7] That way people don't get comfortable and find ways to drag out the session. When this guidance is followed, subteam members will only be spending 15 to 30 minutes per week in review meetings. Subteam leaders will need the information from these meetings to report at the project level progress review meeting. For this reason, it makes sense to schedule subteam review meetings just prior to the project-level review meeting. If the project-level review is on Monday afternoons, ideally, the subteam reviews will occur on Monday mornings.

Six Steps to Develop Individual and Subteam Performance Systems

1. Define the final deliverable (project internal deliverable).

2. List modular subdeliverable, if possible.

3. Define quality requirements for subdeliverable.

4. Define the pace goal, if possible.

5. Define how completed subdeliverables will be tracked.

6. Define how individuals will make short-term commitments.

At the outset of a new project, team leaders will decide if they intend to formally set up performance systems for their subteams. However, the first time a team slips a commitment without early warning, the project manager should require that performance systems be implemented for that subteam. It is the only way to ensure that commitments will be met or that the team will at least be warned of problems ahead of time on labor-intensive deliverables.

Implementation:
Guidance to Follow and Pitfalls to Avoid

Team leaders often ask if they should develop the performance system themselves and require their team to use it, or educate the team on performance systems and involve them in developing the performance system. Both approaches can succeed and both approaches can fail. How performance systems are developed and implemented depends on the relative experience levels of the team leader and the team members, the culture and management style of the larger organization, how long the team has worked together, how much trust the team leader has already earned from the team, etc.

It is the responsibility of managers and team leaders to make sure their team members are working under the three conditions that ensure success:

1. Performers know exactly what they need to accomplish to be successful.

2. Performers have frequent and reliable feedback about whether they are accomplishing their goals.

3. Performers believe that if it is determined they need something to be successful, it will be provided (or the accomplishment required for success will be adjusted).

Nevertheless, there is no one best way to engage a team in using performance systems. If you choose to educate the team and involve them in developing the performance system, there are some guidelines that should be followed. First, it is recommended to tell the team that a performance system will be implemented rather than having them decide for themselves. Given the choice, team members often will choose to stick with the status quo rather than try something new. Second, even when involving the team in designing the system, follow the six development steps and insist that everyone use similar individual tracking tools, at least at the outset. The problem with everyone having a different individual tracking tool is that the subteam leader will have difficulty reading them. This makes it difficult for the subteam leader to check in on individuals and encourage them for being on track.

If you choose to design the system yourself and require the team to use it, you should identify a time period for evaluating your design. Require adherence to the design "as is" during the evaluation period, but then solicit input from the team to see if the system is working and how the team thinks that it could be improved. Once you solicit their response, of course, you need to be willing to reply to them respectfully, even if you do not use all the suggestions. When you impose your own design on the team it is even more important that the team members perceive the performance system as a tool to ensure their success rather than a management information system. Make sure they understand that the information from the system is for them to use and that it will not be used against them. Then you need to be careful to make sure this information is not abused. If the information is used correctly, it should only take a few weeks at most for most of the team to appreciate the benefits of working in a performance system.

The most common argument performers have against individual performance systems is that they don't want to be "micromanaged." They may need help distinguishing between micromanagement—when individuals are told exactly what to do each step of the way, and performance systems—when performers are required to do a good job planning their own work and then held accountable to those plans. Micromanagement breeds resentment, individual performance systems breed reliable performance (and usually increased performer satisfaction).

Check in on Performers Frequently

Individual (and subteam) tracking systems tell performers if they are being successful, but performers still want to know that the team leader knows they are being successful. The rule to remember here is "strive to catch people being successful." The tracking tools make it easy to see when someone is being successful. Look at them several times a week and when you see success, acknowledge it. This is an integral part of the performance system and cannot be overlooked. Sometimes team leaders who have successful performance systems in place with measurable increases in productivity stop checking in on performers because they have "too many other things to do." What could be more important than ensuring that each team member is successfully meeting his or her commitments? Remember, when you don't check in, performers check out of the performance system.

Using Performance Data to Continuously Improve

Teams that fall behind their pace goal after the first few weeks are unlikely to catch up and be successful if they continue doing what they've been doing. Have the team use its own performance data to think about what it needs, or what it could do to pick up the pace. Team members may have noticed that one or two people are producing more than the rest. This information shouldn't be used to punish, but it absolutely can be used to find out if the most productive people have some techniques they can share with the others. Sometimes teams are constrained by their tools. If people need to sit at special workstations to complete subdeliverables, but there are not enough to go around, the team may be unable to meet its commitment. When appropriate, use the pace data to show team leadership that more workstations are needed if the commitment is going to be honored. Having the performance data, and using it to address problems, are what give the team a sense of control. As was listed previously, this is the third necessary condition to ensure each performer is successful.

The best teams don't wait until they are falling behind to use the performance data. They have periodic meetings, maybe monthly, where the team members review the data and talk about what it would take to increase their pace and/or quality of outputs. (It is worth noting that reliable performance data is often a key ingredient missing from continuous improvement efforts.) Unlike progress review meetings, these should be problem solving meetings. For any deliverable on the critical path, exceeding the committed performance could lead to closing some of the gap between the bottom-up commit date and the top-down request date for the overall project. Other learnings may not be applied on the current project but can be used to pull in commitments on future projects. These are scenarios that can help team members get extremely excited about their projects.

One More Pitfall to Avoid

The biggest potential pitfall when implementing any new performance system is to forget to make the principles of performer information systems a way of life. Even if you develop a good subteam performance system, if other systems and tools being used on the project are being used as traditional management information systems, they can quickly extinguish an effective performance system. To use manufacturing as an example, there are production supervisors who have set up excellent performance systems, only to have team members attend larger operational meetings where the focus is on making everyone work as fast as possible and placing blame on individual performers. It is difficult, if not impossible, for these two disparate systems to coexist in the same organization. The same problem can occur on product development projects. Subteam and individual performance systems will always be easier to implement and more successful when the overall project is operating on a project-level performance system as described in Chapter 5.

Implementation Guidance Checklist

- Hold crisp and regular weekly review meetings (remain standing).

- Follow the three reporting rules.

- Have tracking tools posted at workstations.

- Check in frequently (catch people being successful).

- Help team use performance data to improve performance.

Checklist of Pitfalls to Avoid

- Letting review meetings get long or off track

- Not holding each other accountable for following the three reporting rules

- Using a variety of tracking tools which are hard for team leader to read (follow)

- Being too busy to check in frequently

- Exposing team to systems that use performance data against them or hold them accountable for performance to which they did not commit

One final word of caution, sometimes subteam leaders panic because they can't get their team members to make aggressive enough commitments at the outset of a new performance system. When performers are setting cautious goals, it is usually because they've been punished in the past for things they believe were outside of their own control. As you can imagine, responding to this situation by pressuring people to set more aggressive goals will not fix the problem. The only way out of this vicious cycle is for people to begin to believe that the management and information systems can and will be used to help them succeed. This may mean tolerating somewhat conservative goals at the outset. Teams that use performance systems accomplish what they commit to accomplish. Over time, this builds performer confidence in both the systems and in themselves. As performers build confidence and see that they can successfully meet commitments, commitments tend to get more aggressive naturally.

Chapter 9 will explore how this increased confidence has been used by some teams to set and meet extraordinary performance commitments. If you are a team leader or team member, you may want to skip to that chapter immediately. You are now familiar with three meetings, six rules and a few simple tracking tools that support effective project management. The challenge to you now is to implement them. The next chapter is directed mostly at the sponsors of projects. Its purpose is to help project sponsors and general managers ask questions of project teams and respond to the answers in a way that supports excellent project management performance—organization wide.

Summary

■ Subteam-level performance systems are the most reliable way for subteams to know if they are on track to meet their deliverable commitments (especially on labor-intensive deliverables).

■ Project-level and subteam-level progress reviews should be coordinated so that the performance data used to make project-level decisions is accurate and up to date.

■ Upward flowing information about project progress will be unreliable if team members believe that the information might be used to punish some team members.

■ Effective subteam-level performance systems get each individual subteam member working under the following three conditions:
  1. Individuals know exactly what they need to accomplish to be successful.

  2. Individuals have frequent and reliable feedback about whether they are accomplishing it.

  3. Individuals believe that if it is determined they need something to be successful, it will be provided (or the accomplishment required for success will be adjusted).

- The most effective subteam performance systems modularize a specific subteam deliverable (break it down into like subdeliverables) so that the subteam always knows if they are on "pace" to meet its deliverable commitment.

- Weekly subteam progress reviews are where each subteam member makes a personal commitment for what they will complete during the week, and where each also declares last week's personal commitments as done or not done.

- Periodic subteam meetings should utilize subteam performance data to identify and justify improvements that would help the team pick up their pace.

1. William R. Daniels, *Chain Gang: A Simulation for Teaching Breakthrough Systems* (Mill Valley: American Consulting and Training, Inc., 1989).

2. William R. Daniels, *Breakthrough Productivity: Managing for Speed and Flexibility* (Mill Valley: ACT Publishing, 1995).

3. T. J. Esque and Joel McCausland, "Taking Ownership for Transfer: A Management Development Case Study," *Performance Improvement Quarterly,* vol. 10, no. 2 (1997): 116-133.

4. Daniels, *Chain Gang.*

5. Daniels, *Breakthrough Productivity.*

6. T. J. Esque, *Breakthrough Systems Sampler,* Proprietary document of the Intel Corporation (1994).

7. Daniels, *Chain Gang.*

PART III

The Cross-Project
Vicious Cycle

A View from the Top: Cross-Project Management

A common reaction of business managers when first exposed to the methods and tools described in the previous chapters is something like, "I like the part where you check on individual progress weekly, but the part about having the whole team decide when the project will be completed makes me nervous as hell." This is understandable from their view at the top of the organization. Top-down request dates for completing projects are not pulled out of thin air. They are based on the best data available about specific product markets (or on specific requests from the customer, in the case of competitive bidding environments). To disregard that data when making decisions about how to best utilize an organization's pool of project resources would be business suicide. Therefore, it is in the interest of business managers and their organizations to ensure that project managers are factoring business reality into their project plans and decision making. It is also in the organization's interest that project teams execute to their full potential.

This chapter will provide advice to business managers (division managers, marketing managers and others who oversee project-oriented organizations) about maintaining a productive tension between market realities and project execution. Business managers can make or break the success of their organization with decisions they make about how to utilize resources. A major premise of the commitment management approach is that to make good decisions, business managers need timely and accurate data about when (and in the case of new product development, if) specific projects will finish. Equally important to successful project execution is how business managers respond to that data.

Each "go/no-go" decision about a specific project has significant implications for an organization's overall project portfolio (i.e., project list or product roadmap). In other words, each individual project go/no-go decision is really a cross-project decision. This chapter will look at how business managers sometimes inadvertently erode their own ability to make informed cross-project decisions, the impact this has on individual project execution and on project lists and how to restore that ability. Whether cross-project decisions will help or hinder project execution is largely affected by the role business managers play in setting project goals. This chapter begins with a focus on the human dimension of project goal setting and its impact on project performance. The best way to do this is to revisit the product development vicious cycle introduced back in Chapter 1. Since the case in Chapter 1 happens to be from a product development environment, this section will focus on that environment before relating the same points back to a competitive bidding environment.

The Paradox of Project Scheduling

One of the ways that business managers can influence product development teams is by challenging them to produce the next product faster, better and cheaper than each previous one. Studies on task pressure and performance lend credibility to this approach under certain circumstances. As common sense would suggest, productivity is lower when task pressure is very low, and rises considerably as task pressure increases. However, the complete relationship between task pressure (stress) and productivity is represented with an inverted U-shaped curve.[1] Beyond a certain point, increased task pressure reduces productivity. In other words, up to a certain point, challenging goals are perceived by people as challenging; beyond that point, they are perceived as stress inducing and unreasonable. Unfortunately,

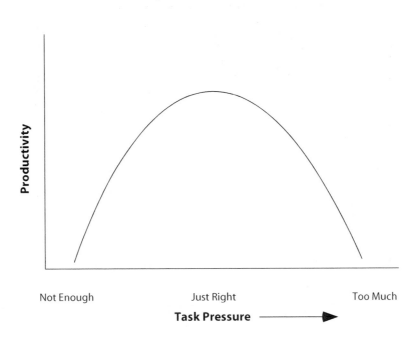

Figure 44. The Relationship Between Task Pressure and Productivity

the graph (Figure 44) only shows a relationship between factors and does not relate how to set just the right goals for a specific project.

Knowing exactly how aggressively to set project goals is difficult. However, the impact that overaggressive top-down goals have on the performance of the product development teams is well understood. Referring back to the vicious cycle in Chapter 1, goals perceived as unreasonable fed a sequence of events that eroded commitment to, and the credibility of, the project schedule. When the schedule loses credibility with team members, updating the schedule becomes a game—the object being to avoid blame at all costs. It is this cycle of events that leads to inevitable late notification that projects have fallen behind and won't deliver on schedule. When schedules slip without early warning, you can count on the fact that the quality of the team's output has slipped as well.

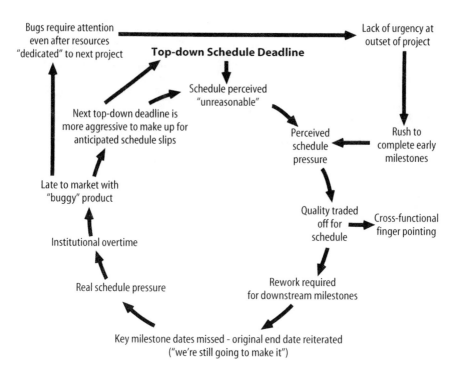

Figure 45. The Project Management Vicious Cycle

So how does a business manager make sure that project goals are aggressive enough but not damagingly overaggressive? The somewhat paradoxical answer is to tolerate two different schedule goals—a top-down or "external schedule goal" and a bottom-up or "internal schedule goal." The external schedule goal is based on what is currently understood about the market window. It is also the goal that is used by marketing to negotiate with potential customers until there is adequate reliable data from the product development team about when they can deliver the product. Because of the inherent uncertainty of complex projects, this is usually not until a project is well underway.

The product development team is holding itself accountable for the internal schedule goal. At the early stages of a project, this schedule will likely not even extend out to the end of the project, which is one reason two schedule goals are needed. The internal schedule goal is what the team has committed to, using a bottom-up planning process. This process (as described in Chapters 3 and 4) considers the external schedule goal, but also considers the best current data about what it will take to accomplish each project milestone. **It is a team's performance against its own committed schedule (the internal schedule goal) that provides the most reliable data about when the product is likely to deliver.**

Let's refer back to the case study in Chapter 1. Ted was given a top-down delivery date and told to meet it. The top-down date dictated an interim milestone (tapeout) date of workweek (WW) 29. Using a rapid and rigorous bottom-up planning process (the team planning meeting), Ted found that the best his team could commit to was a WW 33 tapeout. Rather than just telling his sponsors what they wanted to hear, Ted published a memo stating that the team recognized the external schedule goal of WW 29 and would attempt to find a way to achieve it, AND, they were *committed* to tapeout by WW 33. The most important lesson in the case for business managers is that although Ted's team couldn't find a way to tapeout by WW 29, it did meet its commitment. The commitment represented a 10 percent slip from the external schedule goal, but this was a *40 percent improvement* over typical past performance against external schedule goals. The biggest benefit of "dual schedule goals" wasn't evident until months later, when the product was released for high volume production after one revision instead of the typical three to five revisions. By focusing on its commitment, the team had produced much higher quality than in the past when they were under pressure to meet the external schedule goal. This increased reliability and quality translated into excellent business performance as measured by the product break-even time.

The concept of dual schedule goals is not a new one. One of the best known books about product development, *The Mythical Man-Month*,[2] refers to tracking two different sets of milestones throughout the project. These days the more common scenario in many organizations is holding the team accountable to one top-down determined goal, and then "resetting" that goal one or more times during the project when it is discovered (usually very late in the project) that the top-down goal will be missed. In addition to the obvious impact on credibility with customers and time to market, schedule resets are damaging in at least two ways. First, they erode the internal credibility of all future schedules. People stop complaining that the top-down date is too aggressive, because they know that it is standard operating procedure to reset when the goal is missed. Secondly, schedule resets make it impossible for the organization to ever learn what a realistic schedule might be. It is common for the organization to forget about schedule resets when they are using past project performance to set future schedule goals. This "organizational forgetting" is an insidious way for organizations to deny that they have systemic project execution problems.

One way to think about project goal setting is that external schedule goals are about telling potential customers "what they want to hear" (in order to stay in the hunt for business in a competitive environment). On the other hand, internal schedule goals are required to make sure the project team *doesn't* just tell their sponsors "what they want to hear." This brings us back to the competitive bidding environment. On the surface, dual schedule goals might seem less viable in a competitive bidding environment because a "committed" end date is made to the customer before the project ever starts. But the purpose of this date is the same as the purpose of the external schedule date in the product development environment—to stay in the hunt for the business. It is absolutely in the interest of the bidding organization to hit the committed date. But encouraging the project team to lie about their progress (which is a natural effect of the vicious cycle) in order to keep telling the customer what they want to hear, is highly detrimental to the performance of the project team.

The Cross-Project Vicious Cycle

If your organization adopts the methods promoted in this book, project managers and business managers alike need to acknowledge the value of both bottom-up internal schedule goals and top-down external schedule goals. Applying this dual-goal process may be the only way for organizations to compete in highly competitive markets *and* really know what's going on in each project. Chapters 5 and 6 described what project managers and subteam leaders needed to do to know what's really going on. This chapter looks at what business managers should be asking, and looking for, to know what's really going on across all the projects in the organization.

Just as project managers must constantly manage trade-offs between the scope, time and resources for a given project, business managers must manage trade-offs across all the projects that support an organization's product roadmap. Effective project managers have to be able to say "no" to all but a few requests for project scope and definition changes, and business managers must be able to say "no go" (and sometimes "disband") to certain projects in order to make sure the most important products are a success. Decisions about whether to launch a new project or continue an existing one are some of the highest leveraged decisions that business managers make. One excellent go/no-go decision can cause a domino effect, but so can one poor go/no-go decision. It is imperative that these decisions are made with the best possible data, and one crucial piece of data is whether specific project teams will deliver what they promised, on time.

Many times, the most costly decisions aren't even recognized. This occurs when projects are allowed to continue many months after they are beyond any chance of coming close to their business objectives. The schedule data says that things are going okay, but it becomes apparent that things are not okay just before the final product or a major milestone is supposed to be done. Usually, what is revealed first is that a subteam or two will need just a couple more weeks to complete their milestone. Then a couple of weeks later more bad news becomes apparent. Each time the decision, as presented, is whether or not to continue a project that has slipped its schedule just a few weeks. Usually, the leadership of the team is lobbying to continue the project—they will find a way to "pull it in." So no decision is made (meaning that a decision is made to continue to invest resources).

The real damage from this type of decision-avoidance is that resources continue to be sunk into a "lost cause." Instead, these resources could be used to get a quicker start on the next important product, or to shore up a project that *can* hit its business goals with some carefully applied additional resources. When underperforming projects are allowed to linger, well-performing, and even the most strategic projects, are at risk of becoming starved for resources. Each poorly executed project that is allowed to continue is damaging not only to itself, but, indirectly, to all the other projects in the organization.

At the same time opportunities to wisely cull the project list are being missed, new opportunities are likely being added to the list that stretch limited resources even further. Returning to the product development environment, unless these organizations are very mature and disciplined about sticking to a strategic product "roadmap," the project list will grow as people propose new product ideas that are "too good to pass up." Instead of carefully and rationally honed strategic roadmaps, some product development organizations end up with ever-growing, disconnected project lists. Once every year

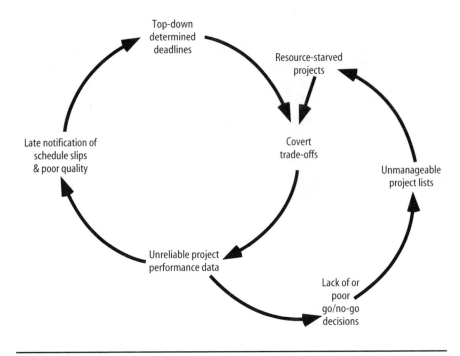

Figure 46. The Cross-Project Vicious Cycle

or two, these organizations go through a painful ritual of purging the project list (and usually fail to purge it sufficiently to ensure their strategic projects are adequately staffed). As shown in the cross-project vicious cycle diagram, the lack of timely and sound go/no-go decisions (at any stage in a project) can drastically reduce the effectiveness of how limited resources are utilized to achieve the organization's business goals.

Another subtle negative impact from this scenario is that projects that perceive themselves as resource-starved are more likely to consider top-down request dates unreasonable. This exacerbates the individual-project vicious cycle and increases the chances that the project team will not accurately report its own status. Escaping the vicious cycle at both levels (individual project and cross project) depends a great deal on the way business managers review project progress.

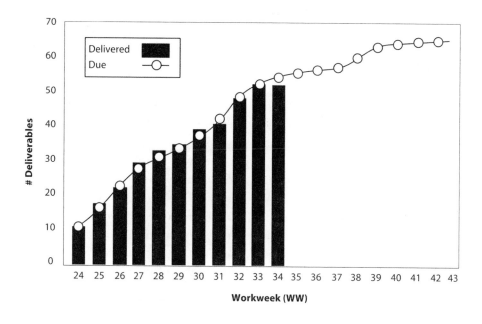

Figure 47. Example of Performance Against Commitment (PAC) Chart

Finding Out What's Really Going On

Although business managers need accurate project performance data to do their job, it is just as important that project teams are generating and using their own performance data to manage their project. Reviewing project progress should not be about monthly or quarterly "dog and pony shows." As discussed in Chapters 5 and 6, project managers should review overall project progress two to four times per month, and subteams should review their progress every week, minimum. Business managers may have a need for formal presentations once a quarter or so, but they can reinforce data integrity and, hence, get good data much more frequently than that. The basic premise of this whole approach is that the way to reinforce data integrity is to focus on what the team has accomplished compared to its internal schedule goal, in other words, performance against commitment. It is recommended that business managers require project managers to keep an updated PAC chart (see Figure 47) on hand that summarizes the number of deliverables committed to be done so far and the number actually done.

Do not confuse this with measures of effort planned and effort completed (usually reported in person hours or person weeks). **The fact that an individual or a team has invested 20 man-weeks into a deliverable that was planned to take 40 man-weeks to complete is not a reliable indication that the task is 50% done.**[3]

In addition to the PAC chart, business managers should also ask for a milestone chart and a risk matrix. The milestone chart (below) shows what is actually completed against both the internal schedule goal and the external schedule goal, but only at the key milestone level. In the early stages of the project, business managers should attend mostly to performance against the internal schedule goals. The key question is: Is the team accomplishing what they committed to accomplish? When teams have a track record of doing what they commit to do, their future commitments have predictive value. These teams have developed a habit of hitting their commitments, and they will very likely continue to do so in the future. If a project is so

Milestone	Internal Schedule Goals (team commit date)	Date Completed	External Schedule Goals (based on top-down request date)
System Design Doc	Workweek 10	Workweek 10	Workweek 7
Feature Description Doc	Workweek 14	Workweek 13	Workweek 12
First Lab Build	Workweek 26		Workweek 23
Alpha Test	Workweek 42		Workweek 38
First Install	Not committed yet		Workweek 48

Figure 48. Partial Milestone Chart for Telephone Switching System

critical that business managers need information between completion of milestones, teams should be asked to institute and report on subteam-level performance systems as described in Chapter 6. Hopefully, most teams will use these systems as a matter of course, but normally, it provides a level of detail below what business managers need to make business decisions.

The risk matrix provides a snapshot of what has been done and what still needs to be done to address the risks on the project (see Chapter 5 for discussion of risk and risk level definitions). When risk is being managed correctly, there should be a relatively short list of project deliverables that are at risk, and the risk matrix should summarize what is being done to reduce that risk. What is most relevant to business managers is whether the team has accomplished what it planned to accomplish as documented on the risk matrix. Teams that are not following their plan to reduce specific risks are more likely to continue missing their risk reduction plans in the future. If these projects operate with tight market windows, they are very unlikely to achieve stated goals.

During the latter stages of the project, the business manager needs to also pay attention to the gap between the internal and external schedule goals. Now the question is, given the latest market data and the data showing when the team will likely deliver (team commit dates), is it worthwhile to continue investing in this project? These are some of the toughest decisions business managers make. The easy road is to let every project continue until it is either successful, comes up against an insurmountable technical barrier or simply fails to hit the market window with a product that customers will buy. However, given the fact that no more than 20 percent (this is the most optimistic estimate) of all new product efforts end up being worthwhile,[4] this is not very good business. In competitive bidding environments, there is little choice but to finish projects that have been committed. The issue here is customer credibility. Would you rather approach a contract renegotiation in anticipation of a problem or after the damage is done?

Canceling Projects

When it is prudent to discontinue a project, the manner in which it is canceled can have major ramifications for how the affected project participants approach their next project. Project teams that have performed reliably against their committed plan (even if the plan was not aggressive enough to warrant finishing the project) should be treated as successful project teams. They should be encouraged for planning and tracking effectively so that the best business decision could be made in a timely fashion. It is to everyone's benefit that this type of behavior continues on the next project, and that the team members approach their next project like winners rather than losers.

What often gets rewarded instead are teams that give late notice that their schedules are slipping and then work horrendous hours so that the "committed" schedule will only slip 30 to 50 percent. In the case study in Chapter 1, the team that turned around its performance and delivered faster with higher quality was at first ignored by senior management in the organization. They were too busy rewarding the teams that were routinely working 70 to 80 hour workweeks to notice that one team was working normal hours, focusing on quality throughout the project and, as a result, finishing sooner and increasing revenues and profitability. It is easy to inadvertently turn sloppy project planning and tracking into heroism. But how often have you seen a team truly *pull in* its schedule by working mandatory 70 to 80 hour workweeks? (Be sure to evaluate this in terms of original project end dates and not reset dates.)

Checklist for Reviewing Project Performance:

- Monitor progress and risk at a high level; let project leaders manage operations.

- Focus on performance against the committed plan (PAC chart, milestone chart and risk matrix); remember, past performance is the best predictor of future performance.

- Praise and reward teams for meeting commitments, not just for working really hard.

Responding to Bad News

When project teams are following the advice in Part II, project reporting should be accurate and this will give business managers the opportunity to make timely business decisions. Teams who were previously operating in the vicious cycle will develop the confidence to commit to more aggressive plans and, hence, increase their chances of business success. However, the accurate news that teams report when using these methods will not always be good news. The way business managers respond to bad news is extremely important in creating an organization that reports accurately.

The first bad news that business managers might receive from a project manager is that the team cannot commit to the external schedule goal. This means that the milestone dates determined by working backwards from the top-down request date are more aggressive than what the team is willing to commit to, based on current assumptions about what it will take to achieve the first few project milestones. Even though business managers feel real pressure from the market, it is in no one's interest to simply demand that the team pull in its commitment. By definition, a top-down demand is not a commitment. The alternative response is to ask the project manager to communicate the assumptions upon which the current commitment is based.

Responsive Questions to Ask:

- What are the assumptions about the project's critical path?

- What are the assumed available resources?

- What are the assumed quality requirements of key deliverables?

- What are the task plans and assumptions for the first couple of milestones?

When these things have been clarified, the business manager may discover that the plan and assumptions have some room for improvement. If the business manager can improve on the plan, or make decisions to change some of the assumptions, then the project manager should go back to the team with those changes and rework the commitment. However, if the team is following the advice in this book, it is more likely that its assumptions are reasonably sound. When that is the case, it would be irrational to expect the team to change its commitment. The business manager should thank the project manager for his or her rigorous planning process and then make the appropriate business decision regarding continuing the project or not.

As previously discussed, these decisions are not based on one project in a vacuum. Each decision to stop or continue, using valued resources on one project, has an impact on the entire project list. There may be an option of "raiding" an existing project and using the resources to start a more strategic one. This is why it is so important that all the projects are held to the same standards of project planning, tracking and reporting.

The second type of bad news is when a team is committed to a plan that is deemed acceptable (reasonably in line with the external schedule goal), but begins missing its commitments. Teams that are not performing according to their own milestone commitments (internal schedule goals) have a problem in their planning, their execution and/or their progress reporting. The project manager is responsible for these issues and senior management needs to ensure these processes are being addressed. A project manager that says, "Don't worry, we'll be pulling in those missed milestones," is not addressing the root of the problem.

Primary Questions Project Leadership Need to Answer about Slipped Commitments:

- Is the team (including leadership) following the three reporting rules outlined in Chapters 5 and 6?

- What is project leadership doing to ensure that future milestone commitments are achieved?

If any part of the team is not following the three reporting rules, performance will continue to be unreliable. If project leadership isn't doing anything to address the missed commitments, there is no reason to expect performance to improve.

Possible Ways for Project Leadership to Improve Performance:

- Improve the planning and commitment-making process.

- Add integrity to progress review practices.

- Elevate issues, remove barriers and/or acquire appropriate additional resources for the team.

Simply telling team members they need to speed up will never yield the desired result. It is worse than doing nothing at all.

If it turns out that the plan is not realistic (the committed plan was too aggressive), the project team needs to replan. Business managers never like to hear that schedules are pushing out; however, it is better to discover this sooner than later. Effective business managers resist the urge to punish project leaders and their teams for admitting that their plans were too aggressive. Fixing whatever it is that is keeping the team from performing reliably to its committed plan should always be encouraged. If the new plan is so discrepant from the external schedule goals that it makes no sense to continue it, now is the time to cancel the project. But that also doesn't warrant punishing the project team (with shows of disappointment in their abilities, for example). If the project goals are unrealistic, they are doing the organization a favor in bringing that out in the open as early as possible.

The Paradox of Control

Business managers have an understandable need to feel a sense of control over those things for which they are responsible. Management is to a large extent about getting and keeping things under control. As we head into the new millennium, one of the harsh realities about business is that it is becoming tougher and tougher to control all the factors required for business success. Projects are becoming too complex to keep everything "under control" at all times. Business managers and project managers that try to have everything under their personal control in this environment are going to have a hard time succeeding and even surviving (lack of control is a well-known source of stress). It is possible that successful business managers need a new way to think about management control.

An alternative to having everything under your personal control is to know that everyone in the organization has his or her part of the big picture under control. Employees like an engineer, product planner or production worker operate with a high level of self-control if they:

- know exactly what they need to accomplish to be
  successful,

- have frequent and reliable feedback about whether
  they are accomplishing it and

- believe that if it is determined they need something to
  be successful, it will be provided (or the accomplishment required for success will be adjusted).

Part II of this book advises project managers and team leaders on how to
instill this sense of control in every project member, and to "roll it up" into
a larger sense of control about the whole project.

**When using this methodology the goal of the business manager (or even
the project manager) is not to control everything but to make sure everyone
is operating in self-control.** Business managers do this by making sure project
managers are operating in control, which is indicated by the extent to which
teams meet their commitments (internal schedule goals). Project managers
operate in control by setting up systems that ensure each subteam and deliverable owner is operating in control, again indicated by consistent meeting
of commitments. Subteam leaders operate in control by setting up systems
that ensure each individual is operating with self-control.

There are at least two significant advantages to having every individual
operating with self-control. First, people operating with a sense of control
tend to hit their commitments. And people who consistently hit their commitments (and know that it is appreciated) are often willing to take on and
consistently hit more aggressive commitments. Second, individuals operating in control, always have some reserve capacity (usually about 20 percent),
and when something "hits the fan," they can use that excess capacity to
regain control.[5] This is the psychology of commitment and control which
is at the heart of why the methods described in this book reliably improve
performance.

Talking about dealing with the control issue another way is one thing, actually changing behaviors is another. Holding a team accountable to its own
commitment rather than a "hoped for" product launch date will take a great
deal of self-control on the part of project leadership and project sponsors.

However the benefits of doing so are numerous:

- Improved break-even-time performance (profitability)

- Improved predictability of when and if projects will be complete

- Better project list (product roadmap) decisions

- More satisfied customers (because of increased predictability and quality)

- Better cooperation from other organizations and outside suppliers

- Less rework

- Improved cooperation between functional groups (less finger pointing)

- Increased retention of talented knowledge workers (because of reduced crunch time)

Business managers that are not ready to commit to encouraging the commitment management approach throughout their organization might want to begin by using the techniques to find out what's really going on with their outside suppliers. Chapter 8 discusses some of the unique challenges associated with supplier management and how the commitment management approach has in some cases been used to improve supplier performance.

Summary

- In order to manage organizational resources effectively, business managers need timely and accurate information about the status of individual projects.

- The project management vicious cycle systematically reduces the integrity of project performance data. When allowed to persist, inaccurate performance data feeds a cross-project vicious cycle that results in the organization's projects perceiving themselves as resource-starved.

- Dual schedule goals is a strategy that has helped teams emerge from these vicious cycles. When using this strategy, business managers acknowledge the need for both internal and external schedule goals.

- The only reliable indicator of whether a project will stay on schedule is the extent to which the team has met its own commitments so far (as measured by the PAC chart).

- The way business managers respond to project performance data (especially bad news) will greatly affect whether project teams can emerge from the vicious cycle.

- An alternative to keeping everything and everyone under your control is to ensure that everyone is operating with self-control. This increases the chances that goals will be met and ensures early warning when goals are in jeopardy.

1. J.E. McGrath, "Settings, Measures and Themes: An Integrative Review of some Research on Social-psychological Factors in Stress". J. E. McGrath (Ed), *Social and Psychological Factors in Stress* (New York: Holt Rinehart and Winston, Inc., 1970).

2. Frederick P. Brooks, *The Mythical Man-Month: Essays on Software Engineering*, Anniversary edition (Reading: Addison Wesley, 1995).

3. Ibid.

4. R. M. McMath and T. Forbes, *What Were They Thinking?* (New York: Random House, Inc., 1998).

5. William R. Daniels, *Chain Gang: A Simulation for Teaching Breakthrough Systems* (Mill Valley: American Consulting and Training, Inc., 1989).

The Unique Challenge of Managing Suppliers

Picture this—Two senior managers are having an expensive dinner. One of the managers represents a company developing and supplying critical manufacturing equipment to the company of the other senior manager. We'll call the supplier Bob and the customer Jim. Bob's company secured a multimillion dollar supplier contract from Jim's company about a year ago. We know who will be picking up the dinner tab.

Bob's first major deliverable was due about two months ago. Bob has told Jim on two previous occasions that it would arrive in just a couple more weeks. This is not the first time Jim has worked with this supplier. In the past, when deliverables were slipping badly, Jim has applied increasingly more pressure (visits by his CEO, threats to cancel the contract, etc.). But the result has always been further slips and often substandard quality. If Jim doesn't find out that schedules are slipping early on, securing a different supplier is not really an option. Jim has decided to alter his approach. He has told Bob that all he really wants is an honest answer in regards to when to expect the deliverable. Also, if he understood what was causing the delays, maybe he (Jim) could do something to help with the next deliverable, which is even more critical to Jim's goals. Each time Jim mentions this, Bob restates that everything is under control. "That first deliverable was an exception, but the next one will be right on time."

Jim persists with his tactics until finally Bob comes clean. "Look, our annual bonus is tied to our delivery performance. If the two of us agree to push out the delivery of your machines, I'm essentially kissing our entire organization's bonuses good-bye." This scenario, based on a true story, is just one example of the inherent difficulties of managing projects across corporate boundaries. Reward structures, corporate cultures, competing contracts, conflicting economic models and a variety of other factors impede the probability that suppliers will satisfy their customers. It is frustrating when suppliers fall short of their promises, but it can be devastating when no one knows that the supplier is floundering until it is expected to deliver. As stated earlier, suppliers that follow through on their commitments simplify the project manager's job a little bit. But suppliers who do not follow through create one more source of project complexity.

It is easy and often cathartic to point fingers at suppliers as the scape-goats for ruining our perfectly good projects. "How could they do that to us? Certainly their management knew that this slip was going to happen and just chose not to warn us." But it's possible that our suppliers are not that much different than ourselves. It should be clear by now that if these suppliers are operating in a vicious cycle environment, then management might not know that slips are imminent on any specific project. Therefore, one way to approach the unique challenges of supplier management is to practice commitment management one step removed.

Commitment Management One Step Removed

Managing suppliers is somewhat analogous to the role of the business manager discussed in Chapter 7. The questions asked, and the way the project or program manager responds to the supplier's answers, can have a huge impact on the supplier's overall performance. On the other hand, while business managers are free to meddle in whatever level of execution detail they care to, it is less appropriate, and potentially a legal problem, for project managers to try and manage suppliers at a detailed level. Luckily, delving into the week-to-week details of supplier projects is not really an effective way to manage them (just as it does not behoove business managers to manage their own project details).

An ideal supplier is one that manages itself very well: confirming when contracted deliverables and key subdeliverables are done, providing early warning when it becomes apparent that deliverables are in jeopardy and working toward trade-offs that get them back on track while addressing the customer's needs. It is recommended that one of your key objectives for managing suppliers is to encourage your suppliers to manage themselves very well.

Rather than asking suppliers for a detailed task-based schedule, consider asking instead for a deliverables map (or matrix) and a risk matrix (as described in Chapter 5). The map doesn't even need to have dates for all deliverables throughout the project at the outset. What you want to track is whether or not the supplier is accomplishing what it planned to accomplish (ideally in the form of a PAC chart). Just as with your own internal project team, the best predictor of whether future deliverables will be on time is if past deliverables were finished on time.

The message this sends to the supplier is that regardless of the practices and rules it uses to manage itself, you will be holding it accountable to at least two of the three reporting rules:

1. Performance data simply shows whether what was committed to be done is done or not.

2. Expect early warning of commitments that may be missed and never punish anyone for providing early warning.

The other reporting rule—*whoever executes the plan generates the performance data that is used to make decisions*—is also worth asking for, but will require some voluntary cooperation on the part of the supplier. Ideally, you would like the supplier to have the owners of each internal deliverable personally and verbally report on their deliverable's status as they come due according to the supplier's deliverables map. It is much less likely that the supplier's team leader responsible for a specific deliverable will tell the customer that something is done when it is not. This level of cooperation probably won't happen until the supplier has bought into the idea that the customer deserves to know whether contracted deliverables are really on track. The supplier's willingness to cooperate to this level will depend a lot on how you respond the first time the supplier provides early warning that a deliverable is in jeopardy.

Responding to Early Warnings

When a supplier warns you ahead of time that a deliverable is in jeopardy of slipping, it is operating within the specified rules and you want the supplier to know you appreciate it. The appropriate response might be something like, "Thanks for the heads up, what is your recovery plan?" Again, the details of the recovery plan should be managed by the supplier, but as the customer you want to make sure there is a set of shared assumptions about appropriate and inappropriate trade-offs. This brings up the important issue of quality. It may be asking too much to insist that the supplier produce documented quality requirements for each of the internal deliverables on the map. However, it is very important that quality be a part of any trade-off discussions. As the customer, you should be very explicit about the quality requirements of customer deliverables (ideally these would already be in the supplier contract) and refer back to these requirements frequently when discussing specific deliverables.

When issues and recovery plans are out in the open (trade-offs are overt), it is sometimes possible for customers to assist suppliers in resolving issues. In the case of Bob and Jim, one of the reasons dates were slipping was because the supplier had run out of floor space for assembling the equipment chassis. This was constraining the number of machines that could be assembled at one time and pushing out delivery dates. In this case, the customer gave the supplier permission to ship partially completed machines and finish them at the customer's site. It was a solution the supplier hadn't considered asking the customer about, but ended up being a win/win solution. These types of solutions are very unlikely to occur when suppliers refuse to acknowledge problems, and the customer's modus operandi is to manage with aggression.

There is a legal argument that the customer should never actually give permission to the supplier to adjust a deliverables schedule. There is no intent to provide legal advice here, but the argument is basically that by letting the customer off the hook for one part of a contract, it may be more difficult to enforce the rest of the contract. You will need to decide for yourself what is more valuable to your project and your organization—the opportunity to take legal action against a supplier or establishment of an open and honest relationship. Undoubtedly there is plenty of gray area in between.

Too Many Early Warnings

Occasional early warnings are much more desirable than late notice that the customer deliverable is way behind schedule. On the other hand, when early warnings become frequent (on more than 15 to 20 percent of reported deliverables), the supplier is not managing itself well. When the supplier has demonstrated that it cannot achieve its own plan, two actions are recommended. First of all, begin to evaluate the impact that this supplier's late delivery will have on your overall project and how to minimize that impact. There is little reason to believe at this point that the supplier will completely recover (at least not without trading off quality). The other recommended action is to ask the supplier to replan. Until it has a plan that it can accomplish with 90 percent reliability or better, it is essentially providing no useful information about what to expect. If this becomes evident, try to remember that the supplier very possibly made its original commitments under the same kinds of pressures as any team operating in the vicious cycle. In other words, no real commitment was ever obtained by the people actually doing the work. The way you respond in this situation may well determine if the supplier begins to emerge from the vicious cycle or if you and your team get drawn into it.

Beware of the "Double Standard"

One way to increase the chance of a cooperative relationship with suppliers is to allow them to participate in your team planning process. In many cases, in order to ensure that the supplier's ultimate deliverable integrates with the deliverables from the rest of the project, some collaboration will be required along the way. What better way to kick off this collaboration than to have the supplier participate in developing the larger project plan. This ensures that the supplier's assumptions get tested and vice versa. It is also a great way to include the supplier in internal deliverable quality requirement conversations.

If you do decide to include suppliers in a team planning meeting, and set reporting expectations as previously discussed, it is important that your internal project team be committed to the commitment management approach. It will be very difficult to hold suppliers accountable to the reporting rules when your own internal team is not following these rules. One software project manager used this type of situation to motivate her team to follow the rules. She explained to her team leaders that she needed them to role model coming to progress reviews ready to report "done or not done" and to provide early warnings so that she could hold the key supplier to that standard. The internal subteam leaders and the supplier's subteam leaders held each other accountable to the reporting rules. When the project was over, the supplier revealed that it was the first time the organization had completed the software portion of this type of project before the hardware.

Considerations for Selection

The first important step to selecting suppliers is to make sure your request for proposals (RFPs) clearly state what you want. Secondly, if you are interested in creating a commitment-based relationship with clients, consider more than price, performance and (proposed) schedule when choosing suppliers. There is an opportunity when selecting suppliers to, as one very experienced project manager puts it, "hire for capability in addition to price." Remember that in the competitive bidding environment, bidders are proposing what they think will win the work, not necessarily what they know they can accomplish. Suppliers that do not think this way probably have little chance of winning the work. But beyond the contract, you are looking for a supplier that has the capability to succeed and the intellectual maturity to be open and honest after the contract negotiations have ended and the project has begun.

One way to find out about these qualities is to research the past performance of candidate suppliers on similar contracts with other customers. Some key things to research would include: on-time delivery, quality of deliverables, safety, ratio of engineers to technicians, etc. This type of research can have a huge payoff for the overall project. Suppliers that have had positive relationships with other clients are much more likely to have one with you. Again, past performance is the most reliable indicator of future performance. For this reason, when you do find good suppliers, it often makes sense to continue using them, rather than putting the next similar job up for bid, hoping to find a low bidder. Along these same lines, when working with new suppliers, the appropriate people should plan some time to build a relationship with them. Joint team planning meetings, for example, are good forums for relationship building.

Suppliers and the Performance Triangle

One way to build a relationship with a supplier is to have lots of up front communication about goals and priorities. Going back to the project triangle, which of the three variables is most important for meeting your project's overall goals: scope, time or resources? Just as it is inappropriate for your sponsor to constrain you on all three variables, you cannot act as if all three variables are constrained for your suppliers. If schedule is what is going to make or break the project, then it will probably be necessary along the way to trade off some cost and/or scope. Trade-offs are inevitably made by suppliers (as by your own team) and it is in your interest that they are made with your priorities in mind.

Returning to the case at the beginning of this chapter, Jim (the customer) eventually found out that his organization had created some of the pain that he was experiencing with Bob (the supplier). When the multimillion dollar contract was first negotiated, Jim's organization sent in their best "hot shot" contract negotiators. These people were rewarded based on their ability to minimize the cost of contracts. Knowing that this contract was a strategic one for Bob's organization, they negotiated very aggressively on cost and were no doubt rewarded for doing so. Unfortunately, the contract dictated so little profit for the supplier from each machine sent to Jim's organization that Bob was delivering the machines to any of his other customers first (where they were making a reasonable profit). Even though Jim's organization was most concerned about schedule, they had inadvertently traded off schedule for cost considerations.

The commitment management approach has been demonstrated to work one step removed, but it is unlikely to work as an afterthought. Suppliers should be selected and contracts should be negotiated with the commitment-based approach in mind.

Part II of the book focused on using commitment management to manage within projects. Part III of the book focused on encouraging commitment management one step removed. Part IV will move into management theory. The next and final chapter of this book explores why commitment management works for those that are interested. Chapter 9 is not required reading. Some of you will be happy just based on the results without explanations about why it works, and that's fine too.

Summary

- Effective supplier management can be hampered by a variety of factors out of the control of the project manager (e.g. reward structures, corporate cultures, contract negotiations, etc.).

- The goal of supplier management is to get suppliers to manage themselves very well. This is done in a way similar to how business managers should manage their own project managers.

- Ask suppliers for a deliverables map (or matrix) and a risk matrix rather than a task-based schedule. This makes it easier to determine if the supplier is accomplishing what it intended to accomplish.

- Only when suppliers feel comfortable being honest about problems does the project manager have any chance of helping them resolve those problems.

- The way suppliers are selected and contracts are negotiated can be a major factor in whether they will be open and honest about their progress.

- Consider inviting representatives from your suppliers to your team planning meetings.

Why This Works

Towards a Benevolent Cycle

The primary objective of this book is to offer an approach to project management that makes life easier for project leadership and project participants in today's highly competitive environments. It is an approach that improves the performance of individual projects and does so in a way that leaves project participants energized and ready for the next challenge. It is also an approach that provides business managers with reliable information so they can allocate resources effectively across all the organization's projects. Hopefully this objective has been achieved in Parts I through III. But for some people this will not be enough. Some people will want to know why this seemingly simplistic method works. That is the objective of this chapter.

Recall from Chapter 1 how business goals are affected by product development teams operating in the vicious cycle. The optimal window for introducing new products is often missed and "break-even time" is pushed out. This opens the door to competition sooner and usually shortens the life cycle of the product. Shorter product lifetimes mean smaller returns.[1] The issues are similar in the competitive bidding environment. Unreliable performance and late delivery bring on additional pressure from customers and a reputation for unreliability that can be difficult to shed.

The vicious cycle erodes quality and morale. Organizations that operate in the vicious cycle tend to lose some of their best talent. No one subjects himself or herself to the vicious cycle indefinitely when they have other choices. On top of all this, the project vicious cycle erodes data integrity and leads to a cross-project vicious cycle that exacerbates the challenge of individual projects by spreading resources too thin. How is it that reestablishing personal commitment can turn all of this around?

Vicious Cycle, Reliable and Breakthrough Performance

To begin to understand why the method described in this book, if implemented correctly, will lead your teams out of the vicious cycle, you need to look to the opposite end of the performance continuum. The opposite of vicious cycle performance is *breakthrough performance.* Occasionally, when the members of a team have decided that settling for typical performance on a given project will lead to an untenable situation (e.g., the end of the organization, being eclipsed by a fierce competitor, certain death, * etc.), a team will commit itself to do the impossible. More precisely it will commit to do what seems impossible based on its own recent past performance.

These teams realize that if they approach the current project the same way they've approached every other one, at best they may improve on their results by 10 or 20 percent. So they ignore past performance and look forward, concentrating on what it would take to avoid an untenable situation. For example, a team that produced silicon chips to control the video processing in a videoconferencing product had been averaging about 22 months to develop these chips. The team was geographically isolated from the rest of its division and received essentially no attention from senior management. When an opportunity arose to become the focal point of the division's flagship product, the team chose to accept the challenge of deliv-

---

* The reference to death is not in jest. Much of the work done on breakthrough performance has been done in the area of workplace safety; for example, helping commercial construction crews break through to a fatality-free workplace.

PERFORMANCE

Vicious Cycle   Reliable   Breakthrough

Figure 49. A Continuum of Project Performance

ering a chip in 13 months—a 70 percent reduction in schedule—with no additional resources. Rick Bair, a consultant in the construction business, has reported on a construction company that challenged itself to build a petrochemical plant at 75 percent of the average industry cost, in 55 percent of the average industry time, in order to distinguish itself from the competition.[2] Alan Sherr, a former IBM fellow, has reported on numerous projects that committed to project goals that would increase productivity by 50 to 100 percent.[3]

Although these occurrences may look to the casual observer as a group of people simply inspired (or scared) into working extraordinarily hard, that is rarely the case. There are in fact certain conditions typically associated with breakthrough performances. The effect of these conditions is somewhat predictable, and it is possible to deliberately engineer these conditions. Breakthrough performance is available to any project team that chooses (in

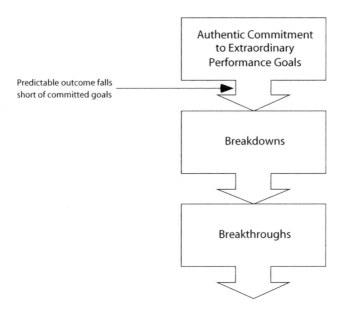

Figure 50. The Breakthrough Framework

Adapted, by permission from Scherr, "Managing for Breakthroughs in Productivity,"
Human Resource Management, Fall 1989, vol. 28, no. 3. Copyright © 1989 Wiley-Liss,
Inc., a division of John Wiley & Sons, Inc.

the active sense) to operate in these conditions. A model for engineering breakthrough performance was documented in 1989 by Alan Scherr, who had successfully set up these conditions with a large number of project teams at IBM. He calls his model the "breakthrough framework."[4]

The outputs of Scherr's model are breakthroughs, which are the necessary components of breakthrough performance. A specific breakthrough is an innovation that allows the team to get back on track to its committed goals. The model points out that breakthrough performance is irrelevant until there is something called a breakdown. Scherr defines breakdowns as "situations where the circumstances are inconsistent with, and fall short of, one's committed goals." A breakdown occurs wherever there is a gap between a committed result and the predictable outcome of the current circumstances."[5] Hence, an innovation—a successful break with current and past strategies—is required to narrow the gap. Simply working harder at the current strategy is not going to suffice. (Note that whenever time is a constraint, you need to be operating in a performance system structure to figure this out in time to act on it.)

According to the model, breakthroughs require breakdowns and breakdowns are much more likely when a project team is completely committed to extraordinary project goals. The commitment to extraordinary performance is required because when teams expect to perform about the same as last time (maximum 10 to 20 percent improvement), they have to perform extremely poorly in order for circumstances to stray far from expectations. When the expected performance always seems in reach, there is no reason to abandon conventional strategies. This is what's happening when teams fall behind but tell themselves they will catch up later (and usually never do).

It should be noted that a breakthrough is not the only possible consequence of a breakdown. The gut reaction of most teams that find themselves in a breakdown situation is to revise their commitment to be more consistent with the current circumstances (i.e., reset the schedule). Doing this resolves the breakdown situation but also eliminates the possibility of a breakthrough performance. The best way to *encourage* a breakthrough is for the team to deliberately choose to stick to its commitment even though it doesn't know how to resolve the breakdown. **It is when the members of a team are authentically committed to a result *and* at a complete loss as to how to achieve that result that breakthroughs happen.**

There is a logical explanation for this. In goal-oriented environments, people don't tend to get creative until they have no other choice. Human beings are incredible learning machines and have a strong inclination to meet goals using the strategies that made them successful in the past. It is only when they have completely given up on past experience to resolve a situation that they become open to all the other possible strategies. Innovation requires ignoring what you already know, and most of us have been trained throughout life not to do that. But when it is finally clear that what made us successful in the past is not going to help under current circumstances, a new world of possibility opens up. Then it is only a matter of time before someone hits on an innovative strategy that resolves the breakdown.

Breakthrough performance requires a great deal more of "inventing the future" than "applying lessons learned" from the past. Because of that, it is rare although not unheard of. If you find it difficult to relate this explanation to your personal experience, think of some historical examples of breakthroughs. The one most referenced in the US is the space program and the goal set in 1961 to put a man on the moon within the decade. There were many breakdowns in the space program throughout the 1960's, the most notable being the Apollo 11 disaster in 1967 which killed three astronauts. But at no time did NASA or its sponsors choose to lower their sights.[6,7] Also worth noting from that example was how the determination to succeed was present each time a breakdown occurred and was resolved. After what those people had been through by 1967, no one and nothing was going to deny them success. And nothing did.

Scherr's breakthrough framework demonstrates that breakthrough performance is not only a possibility, but that specific things can be done to greatly increase its likelihood. The end of this chapter will return to the conditions for breakthrough performance. But first, let's explore what can be learned about escaping the vicious cycle from an understanding of breakthroughs.

Commitment and Reliable Performance

The focus of this book throughout has been not on breakthrough performance but on reliable performance. In the case study in Chapter 1, the team members learned to set reasonable goals and reliably perform according to those goals, or provide early warning when a goal was in jeopardy. Performing this way, they significantly improved their performance against schedule, product quality, employee satisfaction and break-even time. This chapter began with breakthrough performance because Scherr's breakthrough framework sheds valuable light on what enables reliable performance as well. Scherr's model shows that the first condition for breakthrough performance is authentic commitment to the project goals. The first and most important condition for reliable performance is also commitment to project goals.

When teams operate in the vicious cycle, a variety of forces feed on each other to deteriorate project performance. Most of the behaviors in the vicious cycle not only reinforce the next behavior in the cycle, they also erode the commitment of the team to the project goals and project plan (see Figure 51). This lack of commitment is what needs to change in order for teams to emerge from the vicious cycle and perform reliably. One of the key outcomes of following the approach described in this book is to reestablish team commitment to project goals.

Chapter 2 provided an operational definition of commitments, distinguishing

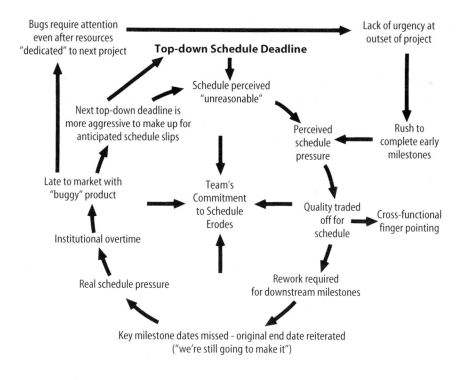

Figure 51. The Vicious Cycle Erodes Commitment to Project Goals

them from estimates and goals. Here we explore what transforms goals and estimates into commitments and why that transformation must happen in order to get out of the vicious cycle. Reestablishing the commitment of the project team to its goals requires "choice, clarity and the rational use of feedback."

Choice

In our operational definition of commitment, the term "personal promise" is technically redundant. It is not possible to make a promise for someone else. It is also not possible to make a promise under duress. Promises are personal choices made without fear of the consequences of not making one choice versus another. When teams are operating in the vicious cycle, their project plans are heavily flavored with a top-down requested end date. Project managers "commit" that the team will "do what it takes to meet the top-down date," because they perceive that they have no other choice. If the team is given the opportunity to have input into the plan, they know that pushing out the end date significantly is not an option. Under these circumstances, the plan that results cannot be a network of commitments. This approach reinforces the vicious cycle.

To perceive that they are making a choice to accept a project plan, each team member needs the opportunity to voice his or her own assumptions about what will make the project a success (either the overall project or specific parts an individual is most concerned about). To test this assertion you can perform a thought experiment. Ask yourself how committed you would be to a project plan if you knew that the current plan was based on poor, or at best, incomplete assumptions. Why would anyone believe that their assumptions have been considered, when he or she was never asked to share those assumptions?

Project assumptions are unlimited in number and scope. There are assumptions about the customer, assumptions about business goals, assumptions about risk and assumptions about how many hours or days certain tasks will take certain individuals. Of course these assumptions will be at various levels of validity. Some will be pure opinion and some will be careful assertions with data provided to back them up. Some will be based on bravado and some will be based on fear. It is important that all team members have the opportunity to share their assumptions and that these assumptions are publicly tested. After discussion, those assumptions that are shared by the key decision makers are the ones that get baked into the plan. The process described in Chapter 4 is designed to help large project teams share and test assumptions in a timely and structured fashion. Team members who participate in such a process are very likely to choose to commit to the resulting plan. The outcome of the process, when done correctly, will be a network of commitments making up the plan.

Clarity
In order to choose to make specific commitments, people need to have either blind faith in themselves and the entire team (which is often a precursor to breakthrough performance), or a clear idea of what it is they are choosing. Teams operating in the vicious cycle are used to failure (schedule slippage, quality escapes, etc.), which doesn't do much for faith in the team. So reestablishing commitment requires absolutely clear goals about which team members can make an informed choice. Clarity requires an understanding of both the pace and the quality of the work required to produce a deliverable. Asking the design team if they can complete "spec writing" in six weeks

is not adequate clarity. Chapters 3 and 4 describe the need to state goals in terms of deliverables and a process for getting clear about the required quality of specific deliverables.

When teams fall prey to the vicious cycle, not only commitment but also trust in each other erodes as well. In these circumstances (always the case for teams operating in the vicious cycle), clarity requires that project commitments be broken down into subteam commitments, and subteam commitments into personal commitments. **Individuals need to be successful meeting commitments they believe they have control over, before making commitments that rely on the performance of the rest of the subteam or the entire project team.** Chapter 6 described how to break deliverables into subdeliverables that individuals can produce in 1 week or less. This is the level of clarity that is required to ensure subteams and individuals are working in performance systems.

Plans made up of estimates of how long it will take subteams to complete tasks, and that fail to specify the quality of subdeliverables with input from the users of those subdeliverables, are not clear enough. And no amount of modeling and manipulating those plans with sophisticated software programs is going to produce reliable performance against those plans. These task estimate plans (in contrast to deliverable/commitment plans) also preclude the ability for the effective use of performance feedback.

Rational Use of Feedback
One of the great distinguishing characteristics of human beings is that we are goal-oriented. Once we make a goal our own (commit to it), we have a great interest in understanding any gap that exists between ourselves and the goal so we can close that gap. The information that helps us characterize the gap at all times is called feedback. Feedback tells us exactly where we stand in respect to where we want to be (the committed goal). The value of feedback is one more reason that clarity is important. If the goal is not clear, then by definition the gap is not clear, and feedback is of limited usefulness.

When operating in the vicious cycle, teams are not committed to the goal so it is not imperative to have accurate information about the gap between the current status and the goal. In fact, it is quite threatening for that information to exist, because in the vicious cycle that information is often used to threaten or punish members of the project team (remember the game of "schedule chicken" mentioned in Chapter 1). As a result, it is quite predictable that teams in the vicious cycle have relatively vague goals, which result in vague feedback, which makes it easy to say, "According to the feedback, progress against the goal looks fine." In this way, no one can prove that individuals or teams are falling behind until very late in the game. Any threats or punishments are postponed until later when it becomes evident that everyone is behind and it is more difficult to place blame. Blame is typically still put on some individuals or groups, but the chances of getting the blame are reduced for each individual.

What was just described is the irrational use (and abuse) of feedback. Chapters 5 and 6 describe the rational use of feedback. As touched on in those chapters, there are two benefits of using feedback rationally. First, armed with accurate feedback, committed individuals, being goal-oriented by nature, are very likely to succeed. Successful projects are made up of numerous successes against individual commitments, leading to many successes against subteam commitments, leading to ultimate success against the projects committed plan. Second, a very rational use of feedback is to immediately "raise a flag" when feedback shows that a commitment is in jeopardy. This allows the team leadership to coordinate work in response to the performance feedback and make overt trade-offs as appropriate.

The word *rational* was chosen very carefully. When every individual operates based on clear commitments and timely feedback, the vast majority of commitments will take care of themselves (although it is still important to monitor them). When someone realizes that a problem exists and provides early warning, the most irrational way that information could possibly be used is to punish the person that raises the flag. This is another good place for a personal thought experiment. Think of an important personal commitment that you made and then struggled with. It could be at work on a project or at home with a friend or relative. How did you feel about the possibility of missing your commitment? What is the worst thing that someone could do to you when you are in that situation? How would you like it if instead of helping you get back on track, someone acted like he or she was more committed to the outcome than you are? People on teams operating in the vicious cycle do this to each other quite frequently—at least until everyone realizes what's happening and starts covering problems up instead of raising the flag.

Building Commitment Muscle (and Mutual Respect)

The previous section identified the individual components or conditions that must be in place to reestablish team commitment to project plans and goals. Two of these components, clear goals and feedback, were already introduced as components of an overall framework—the performance system structure. The distinction between setting goals and securing commitments to goals is what transforms the performance system structure from a "management exercise" into a catalyst for extremely reliable performance. Teams deeply entrenched in the vicious cycle, with all the associated performance problems, can jump to reliable performance at any time by implementing the methods in Part II. However, performance improvement does not need to remain at the level of reliable performance to typical project goals.

The process of sharing assumptions during planning is the first step towards mutual respect and, hence, trust between team members, between subteams and, finally, between managers and employees. The next important step towards trust is when individual commitments are taken seriously and everyone holds themselves accountable to them. Each successfully completed commitment is a statement of personal credibility and a step towards subteam and overall team success. As these successes build up over time, the confidence of the team members also builds—success breeds success.

Teams that have confidence in themselves and their colleagues, and that are well informed of the real business imperatives—market windows, product roadmaps and competing products—often start making more aggressive commitments. Teams working in these conditions will eventually set their own goals as aggressively or more aggressively than management would ever think to impose on them. With some education and careful coaching, they might even choose to set breakthrough project goals. But getting to this stage requires some patience while teams work themselves out of the vicious cycle.

Increasing the trust in an organization is a little like increasing your physical strength. Each commitment met is like a set of push-ups or bench presses. If someone does several sets of push-ups every week, consistently for several months, they will start to see evidence of increased muscle mass. Likewise, teams that manage by consistently making and meeting commitments to deliver project deliverables and subdeliverables, build commitment muscle.

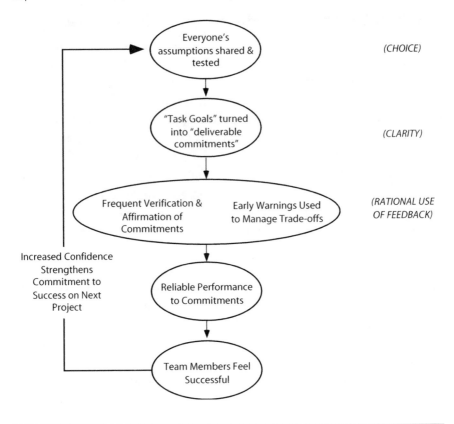

Figure 52. A Benevolent Cycle

The best thing that business managers can do to speed up this process is to provide lots of encouragement for performing to commitments (and for providing early warning when plans have been determined to be too aggressive). Forcing unreasonable deadlines on a project team is like handing a 250 pound barbell to someone who is used to exercising with 100 pounds. In an effort to get project teams to lift as much as they possibly can, business managers are prone to hand out 250 pound barbells.

Changing the Momentum

One of the most important lessons to be learned from the case study in Chapter 1 is that in today's complex work environments, poor project execution is usually not the result of a particularly unskilled project manager or the unwillingness of project participants to rise to the business challenge. The vicious cycle is a systemic problem. It stems from a dynamic that builds up momentum over time, and it is very difficult to observe from the inside (in an organization where the dynamic is evolving). As with any systemic problem, everyone sees a part of the system, and from their individual fragmented views, draws erroneous conclusions about cause and effect.[8]

Now that we have stepped back to view the larger system, it seems that there may be a tremendous opportunity. What if the self-perpetuating momentum of the vicious cycle could be turned in the direction of the other end of the performance spectrum? The observation that "success breeds success" suggests that once momentum is turned around, it will build just as it does in the vicious cycle. The result of getting this momentum moving in the right direction would be a "benevolent cycle" of project performance.

The bridge that links the vicious cycle to the benevolent cycle is commitment. Teams in the vicious cycle have lost commitment to project goals and schedules. As teams begin using commitment management, they learn how to perform reliably again. Integrity is restored to goal setting and reporting, and commitment again builds. Reliable performance, along with excellent leadership, gives some teams the courage to authentically commit to do what they aren't even sure they know how to do. If the commitment momentum in your organization is moving in the wrong direction, there are potentially tremendous benefits to turning that momentum around—towards breakthrough performance.

A Pep Talk Before You Begin

One of the icons of excellent performance in the 1960's and 1970's was the Alabama football team, coached by the legendary "Bear" Bryant. Bryant's teams won 80 percent of their games and six national championships between 1958 to 1982.[9] When the media asked Bryant about the secret of his success, he reveled in painting the picture of himself they so much wanted to see. He talked about the incredible talent and commitment of "his boys" and how his job was simply to motivate them to do their very best week in and week out. One would think from hearing him talk that he spent most of the week in his office and then showed up just before the game to show his love for his boys and give them a rousing pep talk.

One of the few outsiders to penetrate this facade was an equally charismatic educational psychologist at Alabama named Tom Gilbert. Dr. Gilbert would later become known in some circles as the father of human performance technology (HPT). Bryant and Gilbert became friends and one day "the Bear" invited Gilbert to come watch football practice. He even offered to let Gilbert go with him up to the infamous and mysterious tower that stood over the practice field. It was in the tower that Tom learned what was behind all the success of Bear Bryant's football program.

The tower housed two video cameras. The cameras were used to film each player at each position. When the players were not on the practice field, they were watching film of their own performance compared against the film of the best players to ever play their position. Bryant's players knew exactly what excellent performance was, and they were constantly getting reliable feedback about how their personal performance compared to excellent performance. What Bryant's team did on Saturdays (win almost unfailingly) was not a function of his pregame pep talks, it was a function of the managed self-discipline that was exercised consistently, week after week.[10]

The point of *this* little pep talk is that pep talks are not enough to achieve and sustain excellent (or even reliable) performance. Project teams are just as likely to fall into institutionalized crunch time, and then the vicious cycle, even when projects begin with inspiring presentations on once-in-a-lifetime market opportunities. Sustained excellent performance takes the consistent self-discipline of commitment management as described in earlier chapters. The good news is that teams using commitment management for self-discipline won't need institutionalized crunch time in order to be successful. Momentum is building in your organization right now. Will you let it build towards the vicious cycle, or turn it around towards the benevolent one? The choice is yours!

Summary

- Commitment management helps teams perform reliably well in complex environments. Reliable performance is in the middle of a performance spectrum that runs from vicious cycle performance to breakthrough performance.

- Teams exhibiting breakthrough performance make their commitments by looking forward to the challenge rather than backward at recent past performance. These teams first commit to a worthy cause and then figure out how to meet their commitment.

- There is a model for achieving breakthrough performance that also helps explain where creativity and innovation comes from, and why it is often missing from our project teams.

- Reestablishing team commitment requires choice, clarity and the rational use of feedback.

- Teams that have been operating in the vicious cycle will need some time and encouragement to build commitment muscle.

- Teams that work themselves out of the vicious cycle have the opportunity to engage in a benevolent cycle, using commitment as a bridge to extraordinary performance.

1. Charles H. House and Raymond L. Price, "The Return Map: Tracking Product Teams," *Harvard Business Review* (January-February 1991): 92-100.

2. T. J. Esque and R. Bair, "Commitment and Performance" (Presentation at the 1997 Conference of the International Society of Performance Improvement, Anaheim California, April 17, 1997).

3. Allen L. Scherr, "Managing for Breakthroughs in Productivity," *Human Resource Management*, Fall 1989, vol. 28, no. 3: 403-424

4. Ibid.

5. Ibid.

6. Peter R. Bond, *Heroes in Space: From Gagarin to Challenger* (New York: Basil Blackwell, Inc., 1987).

7. William B. Breuer, *Race to the Moon: America's Duel with the Soviets* (Wesport: Praeger Publishers, 1993).

8. P.M. Senge, *The Fifth Discipline: The Art & Practice of the Learning Organization* (New York: Doubleday Currency, 1990).

9. Thomas F. Gilbert and Marilyn F. Gilbert, "The Science of Winning," *Training: The Magazine of Human Resources Development*, August, 1998, vol. 25, no. 8: 33.

10. Ibid.

Appendix 1

The Team Planning Meeting

When to Use a Team Planning Meeting

The small and large group processes described in Chapter 4 can be mixed and matched to accomplish a variety of large-group meeting objectives. However, the combination and sequence described in this appendix is designed specifically for developing commitment-based project plans. If your organization's goal is to address existing vicious cycle behaviors, it is recommended that you distinguish between meetings for developing commitment-based plans and other large group meetings.

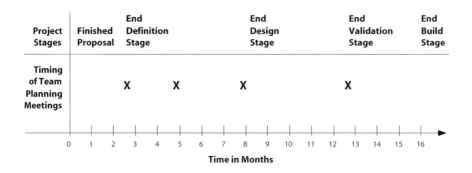

Figure A.1. Recommended Timing for Team Planning Meetings

Initial and Subsequent Team Planning Meetings

After the initial team-planning meeting for a project, the team will not need to generate the deliverables map from scratch. The map can be recreated (or saved from the previous meeting), and agenda can begin with validating the map. For this reason, subsequent team planning meetings can usually be accomplished in five to six hours.

Starting in the Middle

It is not necessary to always begin at the beginning. Teams, already underway, that determine they are in the vicious cycle and want to escape it, can replan their projects using the team planning meeting format. Remember that the team planning meeting is only the foundation. Unless it is followed up by managing commitments through performance systems, these meetings will have only a short-term effect.

Completed Premeeting Checklist

Name of Project	Star
Project Manager	C. Egton
Final Deliverable	Telephone switching system
Key Customer (s)	All local exchange carriers (LEXs)
Success Criteria	• Enable the 4 new identified features • Less than 5% customization required • Meet switching-system roadmap goals
Scope	Out through first full installation
Team Planning- Meeting Objectives	• Introduce 3 new engineers to team • Surface assumptions and move towards shared assumptions • Identify issues and opportunities • Clarify expectations • Build whole team commitment to plan
Team Planning- Meeting Agenda	1. Sponsor presentation 2. Warm-up activity 3. Housekeeping 4. Customer deliverables 5. Internal deliverables 6. Validate the deliverables map (also lessons learned) 7. Internal-deliverable quality criteria 8. First horizon commits 9. Wrap up/next steps
Team Planning- Meeting Roles	Sponsor: A. Reynolds Meeting Leader: C. Egton Facilitator: D. Evans
Preparation Actions (Clarify and Assign Owners)	• Send meeting invitation to all team members (C. Egton) • Have 3-5 key project milestones ready for meeting (H. Su) • Prep sponsor on her role (C. Egton) • Develop list of 10 deliverables and tasks for warm-up exercise (meeting facilitator)
Logistics (Clarify and Assign Owners)	• Reserve offsite meeting room (C. Egton) • Assemble all supplies per list (D. Evans) • Other?

Figure A.2. Premeeting Checklist (example)

Premeeting Checklist

Name of Project	
Project Manager	
Final Deliverable	What will this project team deliver?
Key Customer(s)	To whom will they deliver it?
Success Criteria	2-3 bullets describing how overall project success will be measured
Scope	How much of the project will be planned in this meeting?
Team Planning-Meeting Objectives	Recommended: • Surface assumptions and move towards shared assumptions • Identify issues and opportunities • Clarify expectations • Build whole team commitment to plan
Team Planning-Meeting Agenda	Recommended: 1. Sponsor presentation 2. Warm-up activity 3. Housekeeping 4. Customer deliverables 5. Internal deliverables 6. Validate the deliverables map (also lessons learned) 7. Internal-deliverables quality criteria 8. First horizon commits 9. Wrap up/next steps
Team Planning-Meeting Roles	Sponsor Meeting driver (usually project manager) Facilitator
Preparation Actions (Clarify and Assign Owners)	• Agree on and invite list of attendees (inclusive, not exclusive) • Agree on 3-5 key project milestones • Clarify expectations about meeting prework • Develop list of 10 deliverables and tasks for warm-up exercise • Other?
Logistics (Clarify and Assign Owners)	• Reserve a meeting room that meets criteria (specify room setup) • Assemble all supplies per list Other?

Figure A.3. Premeeting Checklist Template

Team Planning Meeting Logistics

#	Item	Amount
1	Chart paper (e.g. blank newsprint) for deliverables map	6-8 feet wide x 30-50 feet long (can tape 2 three to four-foot-wide pieces together)
2	3x5 inch yellow sticky notes	About 1 pack of 50 per person
3	3x5 inch pink sticky notes	3 packs
4	4x6 inch yellow sticky notes	4 packs
5	4x6 inch pink sticky notes	2 packs
6	Adhesive dots (little round stickers)	1 package
7	Flip chart markers	Two per flip chart
8	Felt tip pens	1 per person

Figure A.4. Materials Checklist

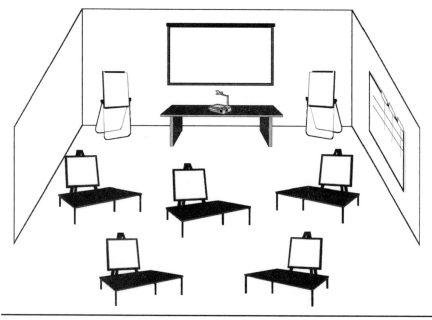

Figure A.5. Room Setup

Item #	Item	Comments
1	Tables should be about 10 feet apart, and 10 feet from walls	Need room for people to work around tables and up at the walls (note: round tables are better than square ones for small group process).
2	Lots of available wall space	The deliverables map requires available wall space 30-60 feet long (depending on scope of project) and 7 or 8 feet high. Also need space to hang up lots of flip charts.
3	1 flip chart per table and 1 or 2 more for facilitator up front	Back up plan is to have some teams work with flip chart paper taped to walls
4	Facilitator should check room setup 30 minutes before meeting begins	Allows time to re-arrange or find missing elements
5	Allow time to prepare the blank Deliverables map before meeting begins.	Allow 15-20 minutes for at least two people to put up the chart paper. Apply the 3-5 milestone reference points. (example below)
6	Coach whoever will be kicking off the meeting	Make sure the speaker plans to cover: • business imperative for project • key customer(s) and ultimate deliverable • high-level project success measures Remind them to keep it brief!
7	Distribute Materials	Per table: 2 packs 3x5 sticky notes and 1 felt tip pen per person.

Figure A.6. Room Setup Checklist

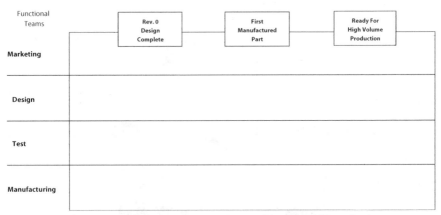

Note: On a construction project, the "Functional Teams" would be the trades (e.g. site prep, plumbing, electrical, etc.).

Figure A.7. Preparing the Deliverables Map

Team Planning Meeting Suggested Agenda

Day 1			
Item	Activity	Outcome	Est. Time
1	Sponsor Presentation	Define customer, ultimate project deliverable and high level success criteria.	15 min.
2	Housekeeping: Warm-Up Activity Meeting Agenda/Roles Ground Rules	Clear expectations for this meeting	45 min.
3	Define Customer Deliverables (Plus Break)	3-7 tangible things we will deliver to the customer(s)	70 min.
4	Define Internal Deliverables (Plus Break)	8-12 major things that must be produced along the way to deliver each customer deliverable	100 min.
5	Validate the Deliverables Map (Parallel Activity: Past Lessons Learned)	Sequence of events: who will deliver what to whom. (What lessons from the past can help us perform better on this project?)	60 min.
Day 2			
6	Walk Through the Map (Plus Break)	Identify holes and disconnects. Identify the rough critical path.	70 min.
7	Define Internal Deliverables Quality Requirements (Plus Break)	How we'll know if each internal deliverable is done and done well	130 min.
8	Make First Horizon Commitments	When teams can commit to deliver specific early deliverables	60 min.
9	Wrap-Up/Next Steps	Issues turned into actions, and expectations about what the team will do with meeting outcomes	30 min.
10	Reconcile First Commits to Top-Down Schedule	The deliverables matrix	varies

Figure A.8. Two-Day Agenda for a Team Planning Meeting (example)

The Three Planning Rules

1. Plans are stated in terms of who is delivering what to whom, and when (deliverables versus tasks).

2. Quality requirements are predefined for each deliverable before dates are committed.

3. Whoever will execute the plan needs to participate in developing the plan.

Team Planning Meeting Facilitator Guide

Please note that throughout Appendix 1, all bracketed text represents instructions and/or explanations that the facilitator will impart to the group

Day 1

Sponsor Presentation   0:00–0:10
While the sponsor is presenting, capture the ultimate deliverable, the customer and how the team's success will be measured on flip charts and post them near the right end of the deliverables map. [One way of thinking of the day is that you are taking a trip. What resides on the right side of the deliverables map is your destination. This meeting will determine how the team agrees to get from here to there.]

Warm-Up Activity (Deliverables vs. Tasks)   0:10–0:35
Desired Outcome
[Each table will produce a flip chart with their answers to the 10 items.]

D = Deliverable
T = Task

1. D   2. T   3. T   4. T   5. etc.

6.   7.   8.   9.   10.

Instructions
1. Show the numbered list of tasks and deliverables prepared for this meeting.

2. [Working together at your tables, try to reach consensus on whether each item is a deliverable or a task. Record your answers on your flip chart. You have three minutes.]

3. Time the activity and give them a one-minute warning after two minutes.

Coaching

If there are groups with less than five items completed after 1.5 minutes, suggest they need to speed up a little. You may be asked to define the terms *deliverable* and *task*. Explain that the definitions will be discussed at the end of the exercise.

Debriefing

1. [The first purpose of this exercise is for you to agree upon rules for distinguishing between deliverables and tasks.]

   - There are no "right" answers.

   - Find an item that not everyone answered the same. Ask one table why they answered the way they did. Paraphrase their rules (e.g. we said "task" because it describes what you need to do, not the desired output).

   - Ask people at a different table why they answered differently, and paraphrase their rule.

   - Repeat this process two to three times until you stop hearing new rules for distinguishing between deliverables and tasks.

   - Reiterate the rules they gave you. The most common rules are:

     - tasks begin with verbs, deliverables are nouns;

     - tasks describe the process, deliverables describe the outcome;

     - deliverables are tangible, tasks are not, and

     - tasks are internal, deliverables go to the customer. (However, for the purposes of the team planning process, we will count internal deliverables as deliverables also.)

2. [The second purpose of this exercise is to make you aware that the way something is written can make it seem more like a deliverable or a task.]

3. [The third purpose is to clarify that you will be focusing almost exclusively on deliverables in this meeting.]

[Why?

- Because you are here to get clear about what needs to get done, not how each person will do his or her job, and

- Because it is easier to get clear about the quality of a deliverable than it is to get clear about the quality of a task. The latter requires watching people do their jobs.

- You want to be able to look at people's outputs and determine if they did what they promised.]

Participant Introductions   (optional)

Only spend time on introductions if there are people in the meeting who don't know other people or their roles on the project. In that case, keep the introductions focused on project roles. Make sure everyone speaks up so everyone can hear—this is good practice for the rest of the meeting.

Meeting Rationale, Outcomes and Agenda   0:35–0:50

Before jumping into the meeting, it is important that the participants have an idea of the desired outcomes and general outline of the meeting. One way to accomplish this is to have everyone read Chapters 3 and 4 before the meeting and then facilitate a small discussion at this point. Another way is for the project manager or facilitator to study the process and present the meeting rationale, outcomes and agenda to the participants.

Rationale

[Everyone who contributes to a project (any project) begins with their own assumptions about what needs to be done and the best way to get from "here to there." The team planning meeting process recognizes this fact and is designed to get everyone's assumptions out in the open and then to move the team towards a set of shared assumptions about how this project will play out.]

[As these assumptions surface, some things will become apparent that previously were only apparent to one or a few people. Some of these things are problems; others are opportunities. In either case, it is valuable to make them known to the project team now, rather than after they have a negative impact or an opportunity has been missed. As issues arise throughout this meeting, the facilitator and/or meeting leader will document them for further review. The meeting is also structured so that participants transform their assumptions into clearer expectations of each other. By the end of the meeting, everyone will know who needs to deliver what to whom, in order to finish this project. However, those expectations will be much clearer for the front end of the project than for the back end.]

[Ultimately, the goal of this meeting is not only to clarify who needs to produce what but to get commitments from each subteam regarding their deliverables and the success of the plan in general. The meeting provides project leadership with an understanding of what the team can commit to and allows it to compare that to the time frames requested by the project sponsor. Based on this first pass, the team (with input from the sponsor) may decide to consider trade-offs that will enable specific teams to pull in their commitments. The final team commitments are what the team will hold itself accountable for while executing the plan.]

[In summary, the team planning meeting has four objectives:

1. to surface assumptions and move towards shared assumptions

2. to surface issues and opportunities

3. to clarify expectations

4. to build whole team commitment to the plan]

Meeting Outcome

[The primary output of the team planning meeting is a matrix that repre-sents the team's commitments. This *deliverables matrix* will be used to monitor the team's progress towards its commitments and to make strategic decisions throughout the project. A partial matrix for this project should be available to the entire team within a few days of this meeting.]

Meeting Agenda

Quickly summarize the meeting agenda. Consider keeping a flip chart of the agenda on the wall to use as a reference point throughout the meeting.

Ground Rules   0:50–1:00

The participants should spend a couple of minutes contracting with each other about how they will behave in order to have a respectful and produc-tive meeting. Common ground rules include: putting pagers and cell phones on vibrate (or better yet, turning them off), returning from breaks on time, one person speaking at a time, speaking so everyone can hear, etc. Three recommended ground rules to add if the participants do not volunteer them are:

- when you hear an assumption you don't share, test it;

- before you test an assumption, seek to understand it; and

- test ideas and assumptions but not the individuals who say them.

This concludes the housekeeping tasks of the meeting and you are now ready to begin planning.

Customer Deliverables   1:00–2:00

The three to seven tangible outputs the team is obligated to deliver to the customer

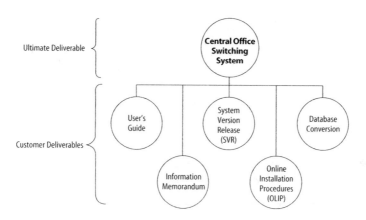

Figure A.9. Customer Deliverables for Telephone Switching System (example)

[If an SVR development team fails to deliver any one of these items in a timely manner, they will not succeed overall.]

Instructions
[To share and combine our individual assumptions about customer deliverables, we will use a process called the *dump and clump.*]

1. [Open one or two packages of sticky notes at each table. Each of you should have a stack of about ten sticky notes.]

2. [Brainstorm to come up with three to seven customer deliverables. (Everyone should be thinking of deliverables from the standpoint of the overall project, not just your individual parts.) Write each customer deliverable you come up with on a separate sticky note.] **(3 min.)**

3. ["Dump" customer deliverables onto the blank flip chart at your tables.] **(2 min.)**

4. [As a group, "clump" like deliverables together. As you do this, be sure and ask each other what you mean by the words on your sticky notes. Test each other's assumptions until you have three to seven discrete clumps that the group agrees are the best.] **(8 min.)**

5. [Agree on a label or name for each clump. Each label should be a specific customer deliverable. Remember to define deliverables and not tasks.] **(4 min.)**

6. [Choose someone at the table who will present the labels to the rest of the participants.] **(1 min.)**

7. [You have 18 minutes to complete this activity. Begin.]

Coaching
Wander around to make sure people are working individually and writing a single deliverable on a sticky note. Some people may still be unclear about whether they should list their personal deliverables or the overall project deliverables. This is usually evidenced by people writing too many sticky notes or by people who aren't writing at all and looking stumped. You may need to refer some people back to the SVR customer deliverables example.

Because this process uses the group intelligence of the entire team, it is not critical that each participant's contribution (or even each group's contribution) be comprehensive. The time limits have been set accordingly. Provide time checks as they finish each step in the process. Make sure everyone participates when they stand up to form their clumps. Remind them that the group's contribution needs to reflect the shared assumptions of everyone at the table. Verify that each group labels its clumps with deliverables instead of tasks. Finally, provide a two-minute warning and then let everyone know when time is up. Don't let groups run beyond the allotted time more than two minutes. The participants need to learn that the meeting is on a strict schedule.

Debriefing

Have one or two flip charts in the front of the room ready to record customer deliverables. Choose one of the groups with an appropriate looking list and have the group leader read off its labels. Record these on a flip chart. Other participants can ask questions for clarification, but they shouldn't be testing assumptions until all groups have reported their lists. The next group only needs to read any new labels from its list—anything not covered by the list from the first group. Continue this process until all the unique customer deliverables from all tables are listed on the front flip chart.

Now it is time to test assumptions. Is everything on the list a deliverable? The group should decide and change tasks to deliverables or delete them. Are these all really customer deliverables? If the list is longer than seven or eight items, can any of the items be grouped together to encompass a single customer deliverable? For example, if one group listed "service-level agreement" and another group listed "product support," maybe these can be grouped into a single high-level customer deliverable.

At this stage of planning, determining customer deliverables is mostly a starting point to find a crisp list of internal deliverables in the next activity. Don't spend more than 20 minutes refining the customer deliverables list. Help the large group make some compromises to shorten the list down to a maximum of seven or eight items. If a small minority is preventing agreement, negotiate a compromise. Say for example, "Let's assume these two items are one customer deliverable for now, and we'll record your concern that they are really separate items. We can check back at the end of the meeting to see if the issue needs further attention."

Break   2:00–2:10

Make sure everyone knows when to return according to a common clock in the room. While the participants are on break, someone needs to set up for the next activity. Each customer deliverable should be written at the top of a flip chart at one of the participant tables (one customer deliverable at each table). The agreed upon list of customer deliverables from the front of the room should then be placed on the right end of the deliverables map on the wall. This list represents a draft version of the team's destination. The project is not over until all of the customer deliverables are complete.

Internal Deliverables   2:10–3:40

The 8 to 12 deliverables that must be produced throughout the project in order for a specific customer deliverable to be completed

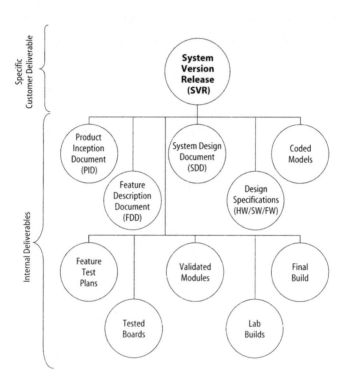

Figure A.10. Internal Deliverables for Telephone Switching System (example)

[The goal of this activity is to identify all the necessary internal deliverables at a high level. A good rule to follow is to limit internal deliverables to 8 to12 for each customer deliverable at this stage. Lower levels of detail can be added later. The customer deliverables and high-level internal deliverables form what we call the *pyramid of deliverables* for the project.]

Instructions

[Unlike customer deliverables that tend to be completed later in the project, internal deliverables start being completed relatively early in the project and continue being produced until they enable the customer deliverables to be produced. For this reason, it is helpful to think in terms of the project sequence of events during this activity. However, think at a high level, and remember to state internal deliverables as deliverables and not tasks.]

[The customer deliverables have been placed around the room on separate flip charts. Get up now and go to a table with a customer deliverable that you want to work on to define internal deliverables. You will all have a chance to look at and test the output of the other groups. There should be at least three people at each table, and no more than ten at any one table.]

The instructions for this activity are very similar to the last activity:

1. [Brainstorm up to 12 internal deliverables required to eventually produce the specific customer deliverable at their table. Write each internal deliverable you come up with on a separate sticky note.] **(3 min.)**

2. ["Dump" internal deliverables onto the blank flip chart at their table.] **(2 min.)**

3. [As a group, "clump" similar internal deliverables together. As you do this, be sure and ask each other what is meant by the words on the sticky notes. Test each other's assumptions until you have 8 to 12 discrete clumps that the group has mostly agreed upon.] **(8 min.)**

4. [Agree on a label (name) for each clump. Each label should be a specific internal deliverable. Remember to define deliverables and not tasks.] **(4 min.)**

5. [This time, instead of writing the label on the flip chart, write it at the top of the larger sticky notes provided. Each group is also responsible for formatting these larger sticky notes as depicted below.] **(2 min.)**

6. [Choose someone at the table to present the information to the rest of the participants.] **(1 min.)**

7. [You have 20 minutes to complete this activity. Begin.]

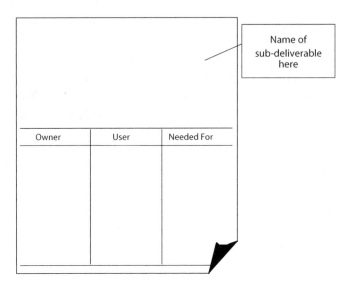

Figure A.11. Internal-Deliverable Sticky Note Format

Coaching
Look for people that are obviously stuck. Use the provided example outcome
for this exercise to clarify what you are looking for in this activity. Provide
time checks just as in the last activity. After the clumping is under way,
provide a stack of the larger (yellow 4x6 inch) sticky notes to someone at
each table. Each internal deliverable will be written at the top of a 4x6 sticky
note, large enough to be read from a few feet away. Each team also needs to
format its 4x6 sticky notes as shown above. Make sure they understand at
the end of this activity they will have 8 to 12 formatted sticky notes each with
a unique internal deliverable at the top and the 3 column headings below.

If the deliverables map on the wall needs any more preparation (e.g. listing
functional groups, milestones or making gridlines), do it while this activity
is under way, because the deliverables map will be used in the debriefing
of this activity.

Debriefing

One at a time, each table needs its selected presenter to stand up and report on the group's list of internal deliverables. Coach other participants to first ask questions for clarification. When they think they understand, then they can test assumptions. Does the list include all the high-level internal deliverables required to produce this customer deliverable? If not, add the ones that are missing. If they have more than 12, would it make sense to group any of their internal deliverables to a higher level? Are they all deliverables, or are there some tasks listed?

When the large group is reasonably happy with the internal deliverables at the first table, instruct the presenter to take the label sticky notes only and place them on the deliverables map. They should be placed in sequence and *at the point that person thinks they should be completed* (relative to the milestone reference points). Referring back to the example, the service planning perspective (SPP), the market analysis and the feature-description document (FDD)—all must be completed before the technical solution can be approved, and they need to be completed in the order shown in the example of internal deliverables. This is a good time to draw everyone's attention to the deliverables map on the wall, just briefly. Review the milestone reference points that have been placed at the top of the template—any questions? Explain that the functional groupings on the left end of the deliverables map are there to keep the plan a little bit organized while it is being constructed. The whole group will validate who really owns what internal deliverables in the next section.

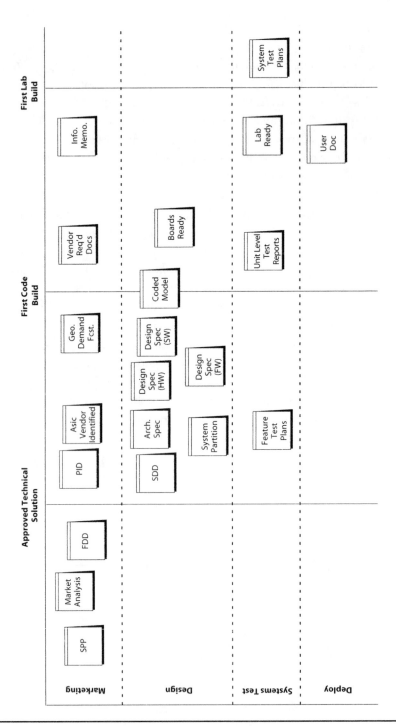

Figure A.12. Placing Sticky Notes on the Deliverables Map

While the presenter from the first group is posting internal deliverables at
the deliverables map, move on to the next presenter. The large group should
be attending to the presenter and not to the person placing sticky notes on
the plan. Continue this until all groups have reported on their internal deliverables. During the break, the last presenters can finish placing their sticky
notes on the deliverables map. It is typical of the high-level plan for a complex
project to have 40 to 60 internal deliverables identified at this time. It is
also typical that more of the internal deliverables will be placed on the front
end and middle of the plan than on the back end.

Break   3:40–3:50
At this point, a very rough plan for producing the customer deliverables is
posted on the wall. The next step is for the entire project team to validate
the plan. Once again, the goal is to allow each project participant to surface
personal assumptions and then move towards a set of shared assumptions
for the whole team.

Validate the Deliverables Map   3:50–4:50
Who delivers what to whom and in what sequence

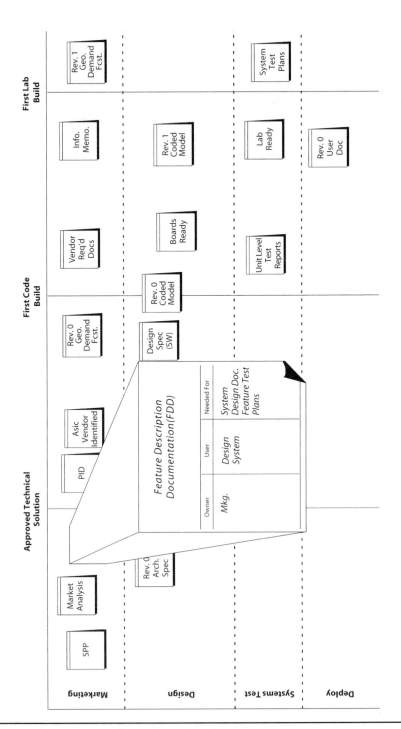

Figure A.13. Validating the Deliverables Map

Instructions

1. [Everyone will validate the map at the same time.* Use felt-tip markers to mark on the map and write neatly so everyone can read it. Everyone should focus on four things in the following sequence:

    a. Find all the internal deliverables you will contribute to and put your name in the owner column. If you are ultimately responsible for this internal deliverable, put an asterisk next to your name. If an internal deliverable you own needs to be broken out into revisions (e.g. Rev. 0, Rev. 1, etc.) you may add revisions to the map at this time.

    b. Find all the internal deliverables you need to do your job and put your name in the user column.

    c. As you are looking for internal deliverables you need to do your job, if internal deliverables you need are missing, add them by creating a new 4x6 pink sticky note (in the same format as the other deliverable sticky notes).

    d. If you run across any internal deliverables that are in the wrong sequence or wish to address other issues, attach a 3x5 sticky note to the internal deliverable in question, describing your issue.]

---

*For teams larger than 35 members, it is advisable to split the group in half and only send one half up to validate the plan at a time. This means you need an activity for the other half of the group while they are not validating the plan. The suggested activity to run in parallel with this one, *Lessons Learned*, is described after the *Debriefing* for this section. Time has already been allotted for running the two activities in parallel. For smaller groups who validate the plan together, you should have about 20 minutes to spare.

2. [Do not move the internal deliverable sticky notes around.]

3. [Do not write anyone else's name on a sticky note].

4. [You should be focused on your own contributions and needs on this project; however, you are welcome to discuss things with your teammates and other project members as needed.]

5. [You have 25 minutes to complete this exercise, at which time, we will validate the plan as a group.]

Coaching

If instructions 1.a.–1.d. are posted somewhere, very little coaching should be required for this exercise. Watch to see that people are following the instructions and have access to the pens and sticky notes they need. If individuals "fall out" of the exercise, check to see that they have contributed to the plan.

About 15 minutes into this activity, the project leader and one or two helpers should start to identify the approximate "critical path" (based on "eyeballing" the plan) at the front (left) end. It is recommended that the "front end" include approximately two to four months of project duration—about as far as team members have a "clear line of sight" to the tasks required (although tasks won't be discussed until later). The little round stickers (adhesive dots) can be placed on appropriate internal deliverables to indicate the critical path.

Lessons Learned   also from 3:50–4:50

Short list of items beyond our immediate control that would make this project better than our last one

Lots of teams conduct some sort of "postmortem" analysis at the end of a project. But these analyses are only useful if they help teams improve on future undertakings. This exercise is designed to take a few key learnings from previous projects and apply them to the present. Most teams will want to focus on what went wrong in the past. More mature teams should be encouraged to also highlight what is worth repeating.

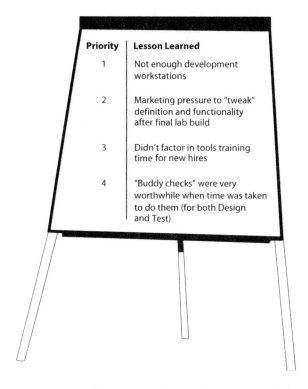

Priority	Lesson Learned
1	Not enough development workstations
2	Marketing pressure to "tweak" definition and functionality after final lab build
3	Didn't factor in tools training time for new hires
4	"Buddy checks" were very worthwhile when time was taken to do them (for both Design and Test)

Figure A.14. Output from Lessons-Learned Exercise (example)

Instructions

While half of the large group is validating the map (group one), the other half (group two) can begin this exercise. After 25 minutes, the two groups should switch and the first group can refine the lessons-learned outcomes.

1. Break the second group into smaller groups of 5-11 people.

2. Have members of each group individually brainstorm lessons learned from previous projects. Remind them that the goal is a short list of issues (or things that worked great before) relevant to the majority of team members.

3. In their small groups, have them dump their ideas onto a flip chart.

4. Clump their ideas and restate them on a clean flip chart. If they have a list longer than five items, they should prioritize and narrow the list down to five.

5. If time allows, have the smaller groups review each other's lists and continue to prioritize towards one list of five items or less.

6. When 25 minutes are up, send the second group to validate the map. Let group one review group two's lists, make additions, then continue to refine and prioritize.

Coaching
Continue to remind the group that the goal is a short list of high priority items.

Debriefing
Before moving on to the quality requirements exercise, instruct everyone that between now and the end of the meeting, each participant should vote on the three lessons learned (using sticky dots) on the list considered highest priority for the success of the overall team.

Sometime before the end of the meeting, the project manager needs to review the lessons learned list and prepare to respond to it during the wrap-up/next-steps portion of the meeting. The response to each item should include:

- the project manager's understanding of the item,

- whether or not he believes that other team members and he can do anything about it and,

- if so, a specific proposed action and commit date.

Day 2

Walk Through the Map   0:00–1:00

Set of shared assumptions about who's delivering what to whom

Please note that this section is the debriefing portion of the Validate-the-Deliverables-Map exercise.

The entire project team should now huddle around the plan, while one person walks and talks through the plan (from the left side) to:

- make sure it is understandable,

- fill in the holes in ownership and usership and

- address any issues.

Another person should be assigned to record issues and actions on a flip chart. Whenever possible, that person should get owners and commit dates assigned to actions before moving on.

If the plan is complex, it is a good idea to walk first through the critical path items on the front end. When the critical path is agreed to, then return to the left side again and walk through the other internal deliverables. When this is done, emphasize to the group that all deliverables are equally critical (required to produce the customer deliverables), but the "critical path" items are more time sensitive than some of the others. They are usually more labor intensive and therefore more difficult to estimate than others as well.

There are 40 minutes allotted for this debriefing. It is possible (or likely) that the walk through will not be completed by that time. This is not a problem. Internal deliverables further than two to four months out do not need to be understood in the same detail as the front end at this time. However, before moving on from validation, ask the group if there are any specific internal deliverables on the back end that need clarification or discussion at this time.

Break   **1:00–1:10**

During this break (or before beginning day two), the project manager and one or two helpers need to select five to eight internal deliverables from the plan (one for each small group table) for use in the quality requirements activity. Use the following selection criteria to pick internal deliverables:

- Focus on the front (left) end of the plan—the first two to four months.

- Use internal deliverables with lots of users. (This means many people depend on this internal deliverable to do their job.)

- Use some, or all, of the front-end critical path.

When five to eight internal deliverables have been selected, put one at the top of each flip chart situated at a small group table. Don't worry about who is sitting where; the project members will have the opportunity to choose where they want to work.

Internal Deliverable Quality Criteria   **1:10–3:10**

How we know internal deliverables are done and done well

Internal Deliverable: Product Name for New SVR

Content:

    External name

    Internal name

Quality:	**Measures:**
External meets marketing Reqs	*Approved by VP of Mrktg*
Internal follows tracking convention	*Loads into tracking system*
Internal uses accurate descriptors	*Descriptors follow naming spec*

Figure A.15. Quality Requirements for "Product Named" Internal Deliverable

This part of the process recognizes that each dependency in a project plan is a customer-supplier relationship. The quality movement teaches that a key component of pleasing your customers is listening to them. In the example, there are probably system administrators among others that are the users of the product name. They need all internal product names to load into the internal tracking systems. Participation in the quality requirement activity would be their opportunity to ensure that the product name is done right the first time. Essentially, this exercise ensures that all the owners of specific internal deliverables know who their users are and that they listen to them before it's too late to do things right the first time.

Instructions

1. [To better define a few of the key internal deliverables from the front end of the plan, look at the internal deliverables listed on the flip charts around the room. Pick one that you are an owner of, or contributor for, and go to that table.] (Give them time to move. It may be necessary to ask some people to move from crowded tables to empty tables.)

2. [Individually, brainstorm content and quality require-ments for the internal deliverable at your table. Consider the best possible quality as well as what could go wrong.] **(3 min.)**

3. [Small groups "dump and clump" requirements at your flip chart. Do this as a group and remember to ask clarifying questions and test each other's assumptions.] **(9 min.)**

4. [Separate the content from the quality requirements and restate each one on a new flip chart page.] **(5 min.)**

5. [If you have time, identify some specific measures for quality requirements.] **(3 min.)**

Coaching

This may be the most difficult activity for people because most teams never have this discussion up front. Watch for individuals and groups that get stuck, and try referring them back to the new-product-name example. Some small groups may want to skip the "dump and clump" and brainstorm directly on the flip chart to help each other out, which is fine as long as they come up with the desired outcome.

For those groups that get as far as identifying measures, guide them to focus on measures that are leading rather than lagging. Leading measures are those that are apparent while the person is doing the work. "Product names must load into the system" is an example. If the person naming the product knows the system requirements, it is within their control to come up with a name that meets those criteria. Lagging measures are those that won't be apparent until the project, or a major phase of the project, is complete. For example, "external product name wins marketing awards" would be a lagging measure. No one will know if the product name wins awards until after the product goes to market. This may be a useful project goal, but it is not the best internal deliverable quality criteria, because it is not really in the control of the people who name the product. Measures must inform owners what they need to do to satisfy their users and ensure their own success.

Towards the end of this activity, put a pile of adhesive dots on each table. Each person will need to have at least 5 dots for his or her use.

Debriefing

[Instead of each table reading out its quality criteria, go to the tables you have an interest in (if you are an owner/contributor or user of that internal deliverable) and approve the stated quality criteria. You will have 15 minutes to do this. Everyone should take a sheet of adhesive dots. If you see a requirement that you disagree with, indicate that on the flip chart with an adhesive dot. If you think a key requirement is missing, add it and then mark your new requirement with a dot. One or two people at each table need to remain there to answer questions. Take turns monitoring your own table so that everyone gets a chance to look at the work on the other internal deliverables. Remember that this is your chance to define what it is you need as a user or what you can realistically provide as an owner.]

After 15 minutes or so, have everyone go back to the table where they began this activity. One at a time, a representative at each table needs to read out loud just those requirements on the flip chart that have adhesive dots next to them. If the requirement in question needs further explanation, ask the person who placed the dot to explain his or her concern. Ask the owners and the users of the particular deliverables to identify themselves. This group should try to resolve the issue. If it cannot be resolved quickly, document the issue and identify who will work on it outside of the meeting and by when. Then move on to the next adhesive dot. Most of the issues were probably resolved during the 15 minute review session, so the whole group should only be spending 5-10 minutes maximum on each internal deliverable. When all the adhesive dots are addressed for a specific internal deliverable, ask the users if they will accept the internal deliverable if it meets the given requirements. Then ask the owners if they can commit to deliver the internal deliverable with those requirements. Again, if there are issues that remain, document them and assign owners to resolve the issues, elevating to management only if they cannot resolve them.

At the end of this activity, everyone has a good understanding of the conversation that needs to take place between the owners and the users of each internal deliverable before work begins on that internal deliverable. There obviously isn't time in this one-day meeting to review every single internal deliverable. Therefore, the owners of each internal deliverable need to take responsibility for ensuring the quality requirement conversation takes place. Have all internal deliverable owners raise their hands and ask them if they can commit to coordinate these conversations with their users. The leadership team (project manager and team leaders) will follow up to verify that these conversations have happened on each deliverable.

Break **3:10–3:20**

During this break, if not done already, the project manager needs to define a list of key internal deliverables for the next exercise. The internal deliverables selected would include the "critical path" items in the first horizon and key internal deliverables in support of that critical path. The project horizon is how far out the performers can see with clarity (define their tasks with reasonable certainty). At the beginning of the project, this is sometimes as short as six weeks, and never longer than four to five months. The actual first horizon will depend on the response from the functional teams in the next exercise. At this point, the intention is simply to focus on the front end of the deliverables map. In the example used so far, the first horizon might go out to the first-code-build milestone. The critical path begins with some marketing documentation and then resides in the design function with the SDD, architecture specification, design specifications and the first revision (Rev. 0) of the coded model.

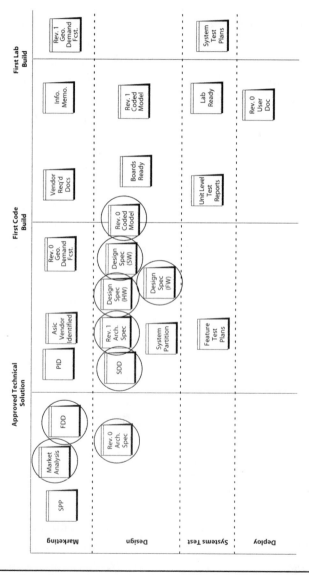

Figure A.16. Identifying Key Internal Deliverables for First Horizon

First Horizon Commits   3:20–4:20

The date the owners commit to deliver an internal deliverable with the specified quality

[There is not time, nor enough available information, to make good commitments for every internal deliverable on the deliverables map, so we will focus on the first project horizon—how far out as you can see with clarity (define your tasks with reasonable certainty). What you should understand by the end of this meeting is whether the team's commitments for the first horizon are roughly in line with the top-down request date for completing this project.]

Deliverable	Team	Commit Date (WW)	In Ballpark?
Market Analysis	Marketing	21	Y
Feature Description Document	Marketing	25	?
System Design Document	Arch/Des	31	Y
Architecture Specification	Arch	33	Y
Design Specification	HW	36	Y
	SW	35	Y
	FW	40	N*
Rev. 0 Coded Model	Design	51	Y

Figure A.17. First Horizon Commits for Telephone Switching System (example)

Instructions
[In your functional teams, for each identified internal deliverable your team owns] (post the list of first-horizon internal deliverables identified during the break):

1. [Identify the key tasks required to complete this
   internal deliverable, according to the quality criteria.]
   (If the team has done some scheduling prework, this
   is the time to refer to it.)

2. [Refer to past history of how long it takes to complete these tasks. (i.e., Will this task be the same on this project? Is it more complex or less complex?)]

3. [Keeping in mind the time constraints on the project] (which should have been discussed in the kick-off presentation), [define a high-confidence estimate of when this internal deliverable will be complete.] (You may need to state it as the number of weeks after completion of a previous internal deliverable.)

4. [Decide if the team is committed to deliver this internal deliverable on this date (remember, a commitment is a promise).]

5. [If not, what would it take for the team to become committed to it (resources, tools, more information, etc.)? Be as specific as possible.]

Coaching

Check to see that all members of each functional team are participating. If not, suggest to that functional group that it find a process that involves everyone, because the commitment should be from every member of the team.

It is possible that one or more teams will conclude that they are not prepared to commit to a date for their second or third major internal deliverable, because they do not feel they have enough information. In this case, advise them to get as specific as they can about what information (or completed internal deliverables) they will need in order to make a commitment. It may turn out that the first horizon, according to the project members, is shorter than what the project leaders thought. They may only be able to make commitments two months out instead of four. What this means is that the team will need to get together again in two months and make commitments for the next horizon. The more uncertainty in the tasks, the shorter the horizon will be. It is better to plan (and replan) more frequently than to pressure people into making bad commitments.

While the functional teams are working on their commit dates, any project leaders that are not participating with a subteam can prepare to close the team planning meeting. They should be prepared to set clear expectations about how the team will use the plan information that comes out of this meeting, including use of the three reporting rules.

If the meeting was large, and parallel activities were used to define lessons learned, one or more of the project leaders needs to prepare to debrief the output from that activity as previously described.

The project manager or facilitator should also create a flip chart that is formatted like the switching system example (Figure A.17) so that the whole group will be able to review the first horizon commits together. (An alternative is to post commit dates on deliverables map as in Figure 22.)

Debriefing

Working down the list of deliverables, ask each functional team to provide their commit dates. If they are unable to commit dates for any specific deliverable, ask them to share what they think they would need to be able to commit. If possible, assign actions and owners to resolve these issues so that it becomes clear when the team will be able to make a commitment. Otherwise, the discussion will need to be held outside of the current meeting, with just the interested parties in attendance.

When all the commitments the teams are ready to make are on the template, or the deliverables map, review it as a group. Are most of the dates roughly in line with the top-down suggested timeline? If not, how far off are they (in terms of days, weeks or months)? Is it only one or two deliverables that are pushing the overall first horizon commit further out than hoped? If so, have the group acknowledge that is the case. Clarify that the teams responsible for these problem deliverables are not "bad teams." The challenge now will be to look for ways to reconcile the bottoms-up commits with the top-down-driven milestone dates and still get the commitment from the team to meet the dates. This may require working through some assumptions, trading off quality requirements or adding some resources, etc. (see the Reconciliation Decision Flow Chart, Figure A.19). If this cannot be accomplished right now with specific subteams, schedule time in the very near future to continue this discussion with them. Consider giving them a day or two to revisit their tasks and assumptions and come up with recommendations for pulling in the commitment.

Meeting Wrap-Up/Next Steps   4:20–4:50

Ensure the next steps are understood by entire team and all issues are turned into action*s with owners and commit dates.*

There are no more new activities for this meeting. However, it is very important to wrap up the meeting in a quality fashion. First, the project manager should review how the outcome of this meeting will be documented and followed up. Figure A.18 is an example of a clean deliverables matrix—the desired end result from a team planning meeting. After the commits for the first horizon have been finalized (again through assumption and trade-off discussions with the appropriate functional teams), they will be published in a deliverables matrix format. At the outset, there will be a weekly meeting to review due and upcoming internal deliverables.

| | Project: | Code Name "Star" | | Ultimate Deliverable: | Switching System (SVR) | | WW: 18 |
| | Project Manager: | C. Egton | | Customer: | AP&P Corp. | | |

Item	Deliverables	Owner	User(s)	Quality Reqs	Commit Date (WW)	Done?	Comments
1	S.P.P.	C.E.	J.P.,M.T.Y.,,T.B.				
2	Market Analysis	J.P.	C.E.	Y	21		
3	F.D.D.	T.Y.	T.B., A.L., N.B.	Y	25		
4	S.D.D.	T.B.	T.B., N.B., B.C., F.Q., A.L.	Y	31		
5	Arch. Spec.	T.B.	A.L., F.Q., C.E., N.B., B.C.	Y	33		
6	P.I.D.	C.E.	C.E.				
7	Feature Test Plans	N.B.	B.C., A.L., F.Q., N.B., D.J.				
8	Design Spec. HW	B.C.	N.B., B.C.	Y			
9	Design Spec. SW	A.L.	N.B., A.L.	Y			
10	Design Spec. FW	F.Q.	N.B., F.Q.	Y			

Figure A.18. Partial Deliverables Matrix for the Telephone Switching System (example)

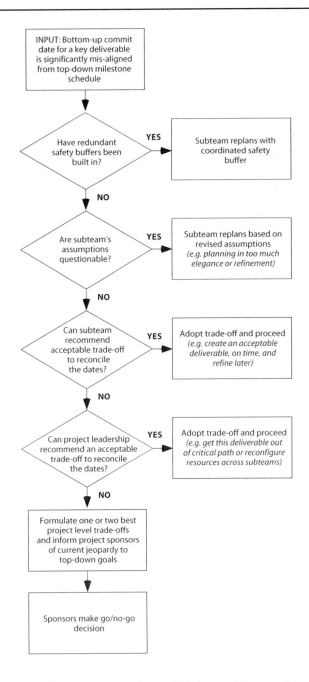

INPUT: Bottom-up commit date for a key deliverable is significantly mis-aligned from top-down milestone schedule

Have redundant safety buffers been built in? — **YES** → Subteam replans with coordinated safety buffer

NO

Are subteam's assumptions questionable? — **YES** → Subteam replans based on revised assumptions *(e.g. planning in too much elegance or refinement)*

NO

Can subteam recommend acceptable trade-off to reconcile the dates? — **YES** → Adopt trade-off and proceed *(e.g. create an acceptable deliverable, on time, and refine later)*

NO

Can project leadership recommend an acceptable trade-off to reconcile the dates? — **YES** → Adopt trade-off and proceed *(e.g. get this deliverable out of critical path or reconfigure resources across subteams)*

NO

Formulate one or two best project level trade-offs and inform project sponsors of current jeopardy to top-down goals

Sponsors make go/no-go decision

GOAL: Get bottom-up date as aligned as possible to top-down date while maintaining subteam commitment.

Figure A.19. Reconciliation Decision Flow Chart

Trade-off Matrix

Fuller[1] suggests that project managers and their sponsors complete the following matrix at the beginning of a new project. This is an excellent tool to begin a conversation with the sponsors when bottom-up commit dates are significantly misaligned from top-down milestone dates.

Consistent with the conversation about the performance triangle in Chapter 4, trying to constrain all three variables would set the team up for failure. Constraining two variables would mean that the third variable would have to be completely unconstrained (unlimited). When there is a clear order of priority, the first priority is constrained, the second priority needs to be optimized and the third priority needs to be negotiable.

	Time	Scope	Resources
Constrain	X		
Optimize			X
Accept		X	

Figure A.20. Trade-off Matrix

Reprinted, by permission, from Fuller's *Managing Performance Improvement Projects.*
Copyright © 1997 by International Society for Performance Improvement.

1. Jim Fuller, *Managing Performance Improvement Projects: Preparing, Planning and Implementing* (San Francisco, CA: Pfeiffer/Jossey Bass Inc., 1997).

Appendix 2

Project-Level Progress Review Meetings

Project-Level Progress Review Suggested Agenda

Item	Activity	Objective	Time
1	Project manager passes down any changes to project scope or business plan.	Ensure project plan is still aligned to business plan.	0-10 min.
2	Review deliverables due this week.	Deliverable owners affirm that they have accomplished what they had committed.	3-12 min. (depends on number due)
3	Three week "look ahead"	Verify that future commitments are on track. Opportunity for deliverable owners to give early warning that they need help.	5-30 min. (depends on number coming due)
4	Review progress on high-risk deliverables.	Anticipate potential "rocks" in the plan.	3-12 min.
5	Review outcomes of action items from previous meetings.	Verify that actions assigned to prevent schedule slips and address potential problems have occurred and have accomplished what was expected.	5-20 min.

Figure A.21. Project-Level Progress Review Adgenda (example)

The Three Reporting Rules

1. Performance data simply shows whether what was committed to be done is done or not.

2. Whoever executes the plan generates the performance data that is used to make decisions.

3. Expect early warning of commitments that may be missed and never punish anyone for providing early warning.

Deliverables Matrix

Project:	Code Name "Star"			Ultimate Deliverable:	Switching System (SVR)		WW: 18
Project Manager:	C. Egton			Customer:	AP&P Corp.		

Item	Deliverables	Owner	User(s)	Quality Reqs	Commit Date (WW)	Done?	Comments
1	S.P.P.	C.E.	J.P.M T.Y., T.B.				
2	Market Analysis	J.P.	C.E.	Y	21		
3	F.D.D.	T.Y.	T.B., A.L., N.B.	Y	25		
4	S.D.D.	T.B.	T.B., N.B., B.C., F.Q., A.L.	Y	31		
5	Arch. Spec.	T.B.	A.L., F.Q., C.E., N.B., B.C.	Y	33		
6	P.I.D.	C.E.	C.E.				
7	Feature Test Plans	N.B.	B.C., A.L., F.Q., N.B., D.J.				
8	Design Spec. HW	B.C.	N.B., B.C.	Y			
9	Design Spec. SW	A.L.	N.B., A.L.	Y			
10	Design Spec. FW	F.Q.	N.B., F.Q.	Y			

Figure A.22. Deliverables Matrix (example)

Project: _____	Ultimate Deliverable: _____				WW: _____		
Project Manager: _____	Customer: _____						

Item	Deliverables	Owner	User(s)	Quality Reqs	Commit Date (WW)	Done?	Comments

Figure A.23. Deliverables Matrix Template

Performance Against Commitment (PAC) Chart

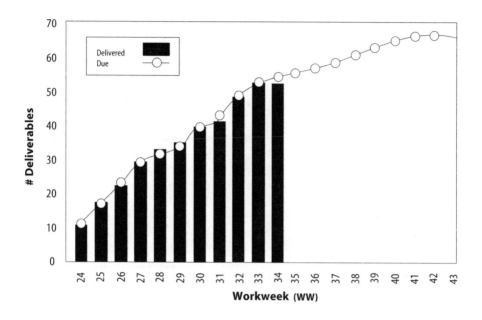

Figure A.24. Performance Against Commitment (PAC) Chart (example)

Milestone Chart

Milestone	Internal Schedule Goals (team commit date)	Date Completed	External Schedule Goals (based on top-down request date)
System Design Doc	Workweek 10	Workweek 10	Workweek 7
Feature Description Doc	Workweek 14	Workweek 13	Workweek 12
First Lab Build	Workweek 26		Workweek 23
Alpha Test	Workweek 42		Workweek 38
First Install	Not committed yet		Workweek 48

Figure A.25. Milestone Chart (example)

Milestone	Internal Schedule Goals *(team commit date)*	Date Completed	External Schedule Goals *(based on top-down request date)*

Figure A.26. Milestone Chart Template

Risk Matrix

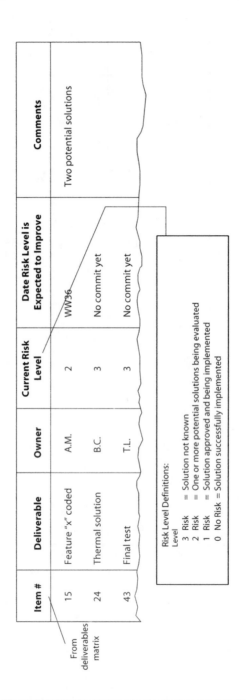

Item #	Deliverable	Owner	Current Risk Level	Date Risk Level is Expected to Improve	Comments
15	Feature "x" coded	A.M.	2	WW36	Two potential solutions
24	Thermal solution	B.C.	3	No commit yet	
43	Final test	T.L.	3	No commit yet	

From deliverables matrix

Risk Level Definitions:
Level
3 Risk   = Solution not known
2 Risk   = One or more potential solutions being evaluated
1 Risk   = Solution approved and being implemented
0 No Risk = Solution successfully implemented

Figure A.27. Risk Matrix (example)

Item #	Deliverable	Owner	Current Risk Level	Date Risk Level is Expected to Improve	Comments

Risk Level Definitions:
Level
3 Risk   = Solution not known
2 Risk   = One or more potential solutions being evaluated
1 Risk   = Solution approved and being implemented
0 No Risk = Solution successfully implemented

Figure A.28. Risk-Matrix Template and Risk Definitions

Early-Warning Report

Early Warning Report

Deliverable: *Coded Model*   Commit Date: *WW 38*

Owner: *A.L.*   Current Date: *WW 35*

What is done so far? *65 of 122 sub-blocks*

Expected completion date without any trade-off: *WW 40*

Expected impact of this date: *will push overall project 2 weeks*

Key Assumptions:
- *validation team says they can remove one week from their testing process if we provide them blocks A-D on time*
- *blocks E-G contain more re-use and will go smoother than A-D*

Recommended trade-offs and/or recovery plan:
Unit test algorithm is creating some idle time. Suggest tools group take a look at it. We can finish an extra 2 sub-blocks a day for every 5% they reduce the run time.

Recommit date with this trade-off: *will provide after tools group implements fix*

Figure A.29. Early-Warning Report (example)

Early Warning Report

Deliverable: _____ Commit Date: _____

Owner: _____ Current Date: _____

What is done so far? _____
_____
_____
_____

Expected completion date without any trade-off: _____

Expected impact of this date: _____
_____
_____
_____

Key Assumptions: _____
_____
_____
_____
_____
_____

Recommended trade-offs and/or recovery plan: _____
_____
_____
_____

Recommit date with this trade-off: _____

Figure A.30. Early-Warning Report Template

Appendix 3

Subteam-Level Progress Review Meetings

Subteam-Level Progress Review Agenda

(Consider holding this meeting standing up)

Item	Activity	Objective	Time*
1	Individual report outs: last week's commitments done or not done	Determine subteam status on in-progress deliverables. Also affirm that team members are meeting personal commitments.	5 min.
2	Team leader review overall progress on in-progress deliverables	Summarize current status, clarify pace that will be needed to stay on track.	5 min.
3	Individual report outs: coming week's personal commitments—team leader may suggest adjusting priorities or resource leveling with subteam commit dates in mind	Keep team members focused on highest priority work. Encourage self-accountability.	5 min.
4	Team leader advises/reminds members of things to keep in mind (e.g. quality requirements, things that will impact hours or coordination, etc.)	Keep important information on people's minds as they head back to plan their work.	5 min.
5	Opens	Immediately share relevant information between team members.	0–10 min.

Figure A.31. Subteam-Level Progress Review Agenda (example)

The Three Reporting Rules

1. Performance data simply shows whether what was committed to be done is done or not.

2. Whoever executes the plan generates the performance data that is used to make decisions.

3. Expect early warning of commitments that may be missed and never punish anyone for providing early warning.

Performance System Design

Step #	Step	Design Element
1	Define the final deliverable (project internal deliverable).	*Coded Model*
2	List modular subdeliverable, if possible.	*Blocks A-G* *Sub-blocks A1-A16, B1-B14, C1-C19, D1-D6, E1-E12, F1- F10, G1-G10*
3	Define quality requirements for subdeliverable.	*Feature coverage, follow code rules, re-use as appropriate, complete buddy checks*
4	Define the pace goal, if possible.	*2 sub-blocks per person per week*
5	Define how completed subdeliverables will be tracked.	*Sub-Block* | *Owner* | *Done?* | *Buddy* | *Reuse i.d.*
6	Define how individuals will make short-term commitments.	*Monday morning meetings*

Figure A.32. Performance System Design (example)

Step #	Step	Design Element
1	Define the final deliverable (project internal deliverable).	
2	List modular subdeliverable, if possible.	
3	Define quality requirements for subdeliverable.	
4	Define the pace goal, if possible.	
5	Define how completed subdeliverables will be tracked.	
6	Define how individuals will make short-term commitments.	

Figure A.33. Performance System Design Template

Appendix 4

Cross-Project Management

Checklist of Cross-Project Management Considerations

Item #	Item	Considerations
1	**Progress Reports to Request From Project Managers**	• Performance Against Commitment (PAC) Chart • Milestone Chart • Risk Matrix

2	**Go/No-Go Decisions (when a team provides early warning that their project is in jeopardy of missing project goals)**	• Test the project teams assumptions:
		  - assumptions about critical path
		  - assumptions about available resources
		  - assumptions about quality
		  - task plans for first couple milestones
		• Ask the team for data-based recommendations and support those recommendations if possible.
		• Explore cross-project solutions and their impact (e.g. pulling resources from another project).
		• Make a decision that doesn't leave one or more projects resource starved. (Avoid the temptation of just telling the team they'll need to work harder—otherwise team members are making trade-offs instead of management.)
		• Thank the team for the early warning.

3	**Encouraging Early Warnings and Data Integrity**	• Implement commitment-based planning and tracking.
		• Role model the 3 Planning Rules and 3 Reporting Rules and expect your project managers to do the same.
		• Remind project managers it is their responsibility to make sure all team members:
		  - know exactly what they need to accomplish to be successful,
		  - have frequent and reliable feedback about whether they are accomplishing it,
		  - believe that if it is determined they need something to be successful, it will be provided (or the accomplishment required for success will be adjusted).

Figure A.34. Checklist of Cross-Project Management Considerations

Checklist of Supplier Management Considerations

Item #	Item	Considerations
1	**Selecting Suppliers**	• Bids that sound too good to be true probably are. • Commitments are based more on a relationship than a contract. • Are suppliers previous customers satisfied? • Overly aggressive contract negotiations may reduce supplier's incentive to perform.
2	**Reviewing Supplier Status**	• Consider involving key suppliers in team planning meeting. • Monitor early and often but in noninvasive ways. • Monitor deliverables—done or not done. • Encourage suppliers for staying on their schedule. • Encourage suppliers to provide early warning of problems and remember not to punish them when they do so. • If possible, have suppliers deliverable owners report on their deliverables. • Beware of the double standard; your own team should be operating with at least as much integrity as you are expecting of your suppliers.

Figure A.35. Checklist of Supplier Management Considerations

Index

Timm J. Esque consults with project teams and organizations to achieve immediate productivity improvements while creating environments for sustaining long-term success. His expertise in project implementation was developed largely during his 15-year career at Intel Corporation. During that time he served as internal performance consultant to more than 30 project teams, especially product development teams anxious to improve their Time to Money performance. His work with these teams was featured in the *Product Development Best Practices Report* and *Training Magazine*. Before founding Esque Consulting in Tempe, AZ in 1998, he held positions of industrial engineer, instructional designer and project manager. Esque has consulted with the University of Phoenix for development of its first Masters of Technology Management curriculum. Timm has contributed to several books and periodicals, is a featured essayist for the Performance Improvement journal, and is coeditor of the book *Getting Results* (HRD Press, 1998). For more information on Esque Consulting go to www.EsqueConsulting.com.

Titles Available from ACT Publishing

In addition to *No Surprises Project Management: A Proven Early Warning System for Staying on Track*, ACT Publishing offers the following titles:

Change-ABLE Organization: Key Management Practices for Speed & Flexibility,
by William R. Daniels and John G. Mathers
$24.95
Describes a proven system of five key management practices that improve cross-functional teamwork. (1997, ISBN 1-882939-02-6)

Breakthrough Performance: Managing for Speed & Flexibility,
by William R. Daniels
$24.95
How to establish an organizational structure where, through resources, expectations and feedback, people doing the job sustain significant performance improvements. (1995, ISBN: 1-882939-01-8)

Group Power I: A Manager's Guide to Using Task-Force Meetings,
by William R. Daniels
$24.95, $39.95 set of Group Power I & II
How to get the best from Task Forces - those groups put together for special, short-term projects. (1986, ISBN: 0-88390-032-7)

Group Power II: A Manager's Guide to Conducting Regular Meetings,
by William R. Daniels
$24.95, $39.95 set of Group Power I & II
How to manage more effectively through regular meetings, where everyone contributes and decisions keep goals in sight to achieve on-time delivery. (1990, ISBN: 0-88390-236-2)

Prices listed are for soft cover. Quantity discounts available.
To order or for more information contact:

ACT Publishing, 655 Redwood Highway, Suite 362, Mill Valley, CA 94941
800/995-6651 • 415/388-6651 • Fax: 415/388-6672 • www.americanconsulting.net
E-mail: Lila@ACTcanoe.com